Scotland the Worst!

Scotland
the Worst!

Joan Burnie

FOREWORD BY
Peter Irvine

ILLUSTRATED BY
Rupert Besley

CANONGATE BOOKS

First published in Great Britain by
Canongate Books Ltd
14 High Street,
Edinburgh EH1 1TE

British Library Cataloguing in Publication Data

A catalogue record for this volume is available on request
from the British Library.

ISBN 0 86241 553 5

Typeset by Palimpsest Book Production Limited,
Polmont, Stirlingshire
Printed and bound in Finland by W.S.O.Y

Contents

Acknowledgements

I should like to thank all those who aided and abetted me in this endeavour. In particular Louis Stott for all those lunches, conversations and large helpings of information, Kenneth Roy, Trevor Royle, Bob Cuddihy, Mary Brennan, Bruce Findlay and Professor Gavin Kennedy for the pleasure of their company, Tom Shields for the elegance of his excuses and Lorraine Fannin for all her suggestions and advice. Even if I didn't always take it.

Some others, for reasons of modesty, if not for fear of their own personal safety, have asked to remain anonymous. But I know who they are and I am duly grateful. Their cheques are not in the post.

And of course everyone at Canongate, especially Jamie Byng, Neville Moir and the incomparable Sheila without whom nothing would have been possible.

Foreword

Having just come off the hill and put down the pen (actually, the mouse) on a revised edition of *Scotland the Best*, I had mixed, perhaps predictable, emotions when Canongate asked me to write this foreword.

Flattered: of course. Who wouldn't be when your idea – not only the concept, but also the style and even the cover – is 'imitated'; that seemed a polite word for it.

Peeved: you can tell. Because *Scotland the Best* isn't just an idea, it's my baby and this new little bastard may belittle or even beat-up on his older brother.

Curious: to see how it would be done. Naming names might be more harsh than merely humorous, an invitation to raise the writ as well as the ire.

And jealous. Not because I hadn't thought of it or written the book myself, but because I imagined that it would be relatively easy; and not expensive. No trailing round the country, up the glen, one hotel/heritage centre/beach after another for Joanie. She'll just knock it out, I thought; good journalists can do that.

All of this before I'd seen the manuscript.

But it would be churlish, petty and bloody-Scottish-minded not to endorse this book. False pride rarely serves us well. Never mind too many chips in our restaurants, it's chips on the shoulder that we should sort out.

The fact is, this book is not the load of old Cobbler I thought it might be; it's written with panache and under-standing, the subject well kent and, dare I suggest, loved. Joan may be what we Scots call a 'nippie sweetie', but actually she hasn't been unkind to anyone and is never sharp just for the sake of it. She has found a path through our crowded battlefields without standing on the corpses.

Scotland the Worst and *Scotland the Best* are not simi-lar, but hopefully our most critical readers, the Scots, will welcome them because both address something that will always preoccupy us – our Scottishness. What is it? Christ and Wallace knows. Fatalism, self-disparagement and pride and then integrity, irony, generosity of spirit and all the debatable characteristics that have made us a formidable race, never mind a nation.

It's all here in Joan Burnie's book – a guided tour and you don't need to go to Scotland.

But if you do, take mine. We are also opportunistic.

Peter Irvine

October 1995

Introduction

This book was born out of a very good lunch which continued into an even better dinner – a restaurant found, but of course, with the help of Peter Irvine's incomparable and inimitable guide, *Scotland the Best*. You scratch my book, Peter and I'll scratch yours.

Over the refreshments it occurred to the gathering that those who are in charge, or who think they are in charge, of this sometimes daft wee country of ours are, just occasionally, inclined to take themselves and us much, much too seriously. Not that Scotland IS any longer merely a country – or at least not according to the Scottish Tourist Board – which has decided that in future the place should be marketed as a 'brand'. Whatever that may be. Scotland is, if nothing else, made up of many brands. All of them different.

Maybe the STB tourocrats will decide which is the real one by visiting our maternity hospitals to burn a tartan tattoo on all genuine Scottish babies' bottoms at birth.

Anyway, even when we all sobered up, it was agreed that although we Scots can, and do, frequently laugh at ourselves, among ourselves, we are at the same time paranoid about those people, especially anyone who lives on the wrong side of Hadrian's Wall, who don't take us and all our works and institutions very seriously indeed. After all, as has been said, the Scots are a perfectly balanced people – with chips on BOTH their shoulders.

A country, a nation, which cannot publicly acknowledge that not everything in its historical, cultural and contemporary gardens, is, or always, has been lovely, is an immature and insecure country as well as a rather sad one. We mustn't always unthinkingly believe our own publicity, good or bad, anymore than our myths. The sun does not always shine, nor does the rain continually fall. We can fail as well as succeed.

This book attempts to tell some truths, some stories and some facts. I hope it amuses and entertains although it may also annoy and irritate because, despite the help and encouragement I had from everyone, it is in the end, only my interpretations and my opinions. I am the sole suspect. This is my Scotland. But it is surely only sensible to accept that the thistle is not only a very beautiful flower but also an extremely prickly plant. Grasping it firmly can draw blood. However its roots are strong and will not be damaged by the occasional swipe.

So for good or ill: 'Here's tae us, wha's like us' – damn few and they're all deadly dull!

Scotland: What the Critics Say

Dr Johnson
(to Boswell when he explained that he couldn't help coming from Scotland) 'That sir, I find, is what a very great many of your countrymen cannot help!'

'The noblest prospect a Scotsman ever sees is the high road that leads to England.'

'Much may be made of a Scotchman – if he is caught young enough.'

'The Scots learning is like bread in a besieged town: every man gets a little but no man gets enough.'

'Oats is the grain which in England is generally given to horses – In Scotland it supports the people.'

John Adams
(on his fellow Senator Alexander Hamilton) 'The bastard brat of a Scotch peddler.'

Winston Churchill
(on Ramsay MacDonald) 'When I was a child I was taken to Barnum's circus which contained an exhibition of freaks and monstrosities but the exhibit I most desired to see was described as, "The Boneless Wonder". My parents judged that would be too revolting and demoralising for my youthful eyes and I have waited 50 years to see the Boneless Wonder sitting on the Treasury Bench.'

P.G. Wodehouse
'It's never difficult to distinguish between a Scotsman with a grievance and a ray of sunshine.'

Francis Locke
'Everybody of that country with any sense leaves it as fast as he can.'

Sydney Smith
'It requires a surgical operation to get a joke well into Scotch understanding.'

Ogden Nash
'No McTavish is ever lavish.'

Stephen Fry
'They called the game golf because they were Scottish and revelled in meaningless Celtic noises in the back of the throat.'

Edward I
'Scotland wasn't worth a turd.'

Tourism and Tartan, Etc.

Despite the best and the worst effects of the Scottish Tourist Board (STB for short), the Scots are not terribly good at tourism. It does not come easily to us. I blame the Vikings. Not to mention the Picts, the Romans and the English. All those filthy foreigners forever attempting to take over and invade the place have obviously made deep impressions on our psyche and sickened us for the trade. However, we try, or at least some of us do, to present our country in its own bonnie licht. Scotland, at least in tourism and marketing circles, is no longer a country at all, but a brand – something palatable and tangible which can easily be packaged, bought and sold. Unfortunately some people, not least those who write books, seem unaware of this. I mean there is the STB doing its damnedest to promote Brand Scotland and a demi-Eden, a veritable paradise and promised land. On the other hand, James Kelman and William McIlvanney and Jeff Torrington et al write their tomes and make the place sound like Hell-on-earth. Worse, much worse, all their books sell and win prestigious and well-publicised prizes. These writers should be banned. Irvine Welsh, who at one point had three books which occupied the top three places in the Scottish bestseller list (and all of them looking at our land through mud-coloured spectacles) could also be eliminated or sent South.

There is also that Gold Blend coffee ad. It takes off where the writers stop, with its image of Scotland as a land permanently washed by rain.

And then there are the midges.

In fact the genus has over 30 varieties but there is only one, the *culicoides impunctatus*, which haunts our wee bit hill and glen . . . and gardens and rivers and moors which should win, fangs-down the worst wildlife title. If this book was sponsored by the STB it would.

But give me the beasties any day against the grouse, sacred cow of the shooting classes in whose name and protection of (at least until it's big enough to fly and die

for its country) countless other wildlife, indigenous wildlife from eagles to fox have been, and still are, ruthlessly trapped and slaughtered.

Worst Date in the Tourist Calendar

The Glorious Twelfth for all the obvious reasons.

Worst Welcome

Those venturing into Scotland's wilder places shouldn't be surprised if they find themselves no more welcome than Edward I to William Wallace.

This is not necessarily on account of any anti-Anglo or all foreigner sentiments. It has more to do with the fact that sizable sections of the countryside are owned by those who think the only two-legged creatures which have the right to roam their acres are grouse and other birds.

Although, to be fair, they seem to be equally willing to take pot shots at everyone, including the homo saps who end up on what they perceive to be their exclusive territory. They also plant Keep Out signs with even more fervour than the Forestry plant fir trees.

And none more so than the Bramwells who own 5000-odd acres some five miles north of Ullapool in Wester Ross. Once it was a popular spot for tourists and locals to walk and roam.

But in 1986 it was bought by Jean and Lionel Bramwell who run an English construction company and who immediately began constructing a plethora of steel gates, barbed wire fences and of course those ubiquitous Keep Out signs. The Bramwells also blocked off access to every possible public footpath and car park.

To such an extent that when an elderly lady broke her

arm while out walking, perfectly legally on ground which could only be reached via a locked gate on their land, it was impossible to get her an ambulance because no-one could be found with the key or the authority to jemmy the locks.

It is all quite within the letter of the law. Although it goes completely against its spirit as well as local custom and does damn all for the local tourist industry. Or the reputation of landowners.

~~Worst Tourist~~ BEST JAPANESE Welcome (Lowlands)

It was in Glasgow. A Japanese gentleman was in search of Scottish hospitality; and George Square. Clutching his phrasebook he stopped a passer-by and asked the way. The wee man took a fag end out of his mouth and smiled and said, 'You found Pearl Harbour easy enough Pal. Find George Square your f****** self.'

Worst Tourist Attractions

It was Fort Augustus according to Wordsworth, closely followed by Fort William. But then the poet never lived to do the Rab C Nesbitt tour of Govan.

However I shall begin right at the beginning – at Gretna: and in particular at its Wedding Centre. Or Centres. There is the new, official, purpose-built Registry Office which has recently replaced the old one which shared a waiting room with the local dentist. It was never entirely clear whether its incumbents were there for a filling or a wedding. Their expressions were equally glum. It was a decidedly grim little hole. But it is not as grim as the ersatz Blacksmithies where fake marriages are held over the anvil.

There are two of those wedding hells which, if nothing else do at least prove that anything the Little Chapel in the Valley in Las Vegas can do, we can do – worse.

Gretna manages to create the least favourable impression of a country at its principal point of entry. Some, possibly Settlerwatch, have suggested its *raison d'être* is to repel all travellers.

Unfortunately it doesn't always work and make tourists beg their bus drivers to go back over the Border immediately and take them home.

Some go on to Aviemore.

In the 'sixties I am sure it seemed an absolutely spiffing idea to develop a purpose-built holiday centre right in the heart of the Highlands. The reality has been a little different – an open sore or even sewer of the concrete brutal school of architecture.

It has given much-needed employment to the area – it's just a pity that most of it has gone to Scandinavian and Austrian ski-instructors, together with bar and hotel work for that great army of itinerant Antipodean backpackers.

Despite everything that has been flung at it (and pretty much everything has, including for a time an incredibly tacky all-year-round Santa Claus land) the glorious scenery transcends and even overpowers it all. On a sunny day.

The same could be said for Edinburgh. I have a vision that on the Day of Judgement I shall drive down the Royal Mile in Edinburgh in a tank and zap every 'Olde Tartan Gifte Shoppe' in the street.

Still, for reasons which are not entirely clear, a recent survey of the place considered most depressing and least loved in Scotland by its inhabitants, came up with Muirkirk in Ayrshire. Let them go to Gretna and Aviemore and they'll soon feel better about their home town. I guarantee it.

Worst Weather

Do not go to the top of Ben Nevis without your long johns. Its annual mean temperature is 31.5°F and the thermometer has been known to drop to –17°F. But on the flat, as it were, the coldest temperatures are around Braemar. These temperatures are not the result, as alleged, of measurements taken immediately following a visit of Princess Diana to Prince Charles at Balmoral, but are taken from records dated February 1895. Every year there are an average of sixty-one days on which snow lies at Braemar, although Dalwhinnie manages even more, with sixty-four sledging days. You will be hard-pressed to manage much of a suntan in Lerwick which only gets around one-thousand hours of the shiny stuff a year.

I shouldn't recommend Paisley either, which lives under a permanent cloud. Not only as it has become Scotland's Chicago (at least in the press) on account of its drug wars but also for its lack of sun. They say that when you can't see the Cross, it's raining and when you can, it's just about to start. All that and the bullets falling too.

It also rains on Islay. In 1923 it managed to chuck it down on eighty-nine consecutive days between August and

Maybe you're right.
Perhaps it is a U.F.O.

November. Loch Quoich does even better. In every year, on every day, it can almost be guaranteed to pour. Except when it is hailing. Its annual rainfall is a nice round 400 mm. It is possible for there to be rain at Loch Quoich, even when everywhere else all around it is sunny and bright. They have a name for this phenomenon. This Highland Mist triangle, as it were, in which everything that enters its environs drowns, is known as the Cluanie Curtain. Meanwhile the longest absolute drought ever recorded (at least until 1995, the data for which is still being collated) was at Fort William where thirty-eight days went by without a single drop of moisture falling from the clear blue skies.

Don't go to Stornoway without tying everything down. On average it has forty-four days with full scale gales.

Worst Mirage

Should you ever chance to meet Llamas in Caithness – of the four-rather than the two-legged species – carrying bright blue coolboxes, you are not suffering from the *DT's* and a too liberal helping of the national drink. It is merely the latest tourist scam from the Kingspark Llama farm at Berriedale which hires out its animals as upmarket pack animals.

If only R.L.S. had been alive to travel with them . . .

Worst Bogs

Even if desperate do not use the gorse bushes – so do the midges – unless it's a choice between those bushes or the public loos at Ardrishaig, which for some reason or other share their home with the local bus-station.

Mind you, many have said that the gorse bushes are slightly better than Pierre Victoire's loos in Edinburgh's Union Street which have combined their store-room with the Ladies'?

Congratulations to the Speaker's Corner Bar and Bistro in Sauchiehall Street, Glasgow which has a machine in their Powder Room which dispenses, for two quid, a pack containing two tampons, two condoms and four paracetamol. After that you are ready for anything . . .

Worst Accommodation

According to *An Australian's Guide to Britain*, 'Glasgow is not well supplied with good accommodation and in any case is not worthy of an overnight stay. However a visit of a few hours will probably be judged worthwhile.'

The man from Japan should have borrowed a copy (*see* Worst Tourist Welcome, Lowlands p.3).

Worst B and B

'Glasgow's most successful hotel' has high room occupancy rates. 'Our residents are carefully vetted and always arrive with a Police escort. Customers are obviously happy with the service because they return with astonishing regularity, sometimes bringing friends and family with them.'

Unfortunately this recommendation came from one Robbie Glen talking about Barlinnie Prison of which he was then Deputy Governor.

Worst Tourist Myth

The Loch Ness Monster is in fact a very good thing. If it didn't exist we would have to invent one.

Single-flipperedly, this animal has brought much prosperity to his patch of the Highlands . . . to Taiwan and China too, who manufacture more of Nessie's souvenirs than we do.

Furthermore where would any (especially the EBC – the *English*) Broadcasting Corporation be without Nessie to prove that they *do* cover Scottish stories in depth?

Nessie was captured in July 1995 – not on film or by sonar but by the American *Sun* newspaper whose front page splash even contained a photograph of the beastie being hauled up from the deep in a net.

Apparently the deed was done by a crack troop of paratroopers and US Marines who joined forces and in a daring raid on the animal's lair, managed to insert a three foot long tranquiliser in its rump.

Nessie was then taken to a top-secret underwater pen at Drumnadrochit for medical tests and experiments.

But the STB need not worry, the *Sun* also revealed that the monster has plenty of relatives.

Indeed when the soldiers went down to capture Nessie, they had to drive them off with electric prods.

So that's all right. There will still be something left for the Japanese and the rest to film if they can't find that cage in Drumnadrochit.

The Editor of the *Sun* when questioned on the veracity of this story explained that they might have taken a few liberties here and there with the actuality but that they did most firmly believe Nessie to be real. As if we ever doubted it.

But just in case, two weeks after the paper's scoop submariners on the Loch reported hearing through their sonar the sounds of grunting and groaning.

Worst Tourist Trap

Don't go to Ballantrae. Few do, even RLS's book wasn't really set in the Ayrshire fishing village but in another place altogether – Borgue, in Kirkudbright. But Stephenson's lyrical ear felt that somehow 'The Master of Borgue', didn't sound as sweet as 'The Master of Ballantrae.'

But of course there are other reasons to avoid that part of Ayrshire including Traffic Police who in the days when the RAC Rally passed through used to regularly charge the competitors for speeding.

There is also the cave, inhabited in the late 13th century by the cannibal Sawney Bean and his family who were also given to stopping travellers on local roads and turning them into kebabs.

Worst Tourist Attractions (Nearly)

When Mel Gibson decided to hold the European premiere of *Braveheart*, his movie about Wallace, in Stirling, he wanted something really special to mark the event. So he sought permission to build, at the foot of the Wallace memorial, a replica of the fort used in his film. Sadly, his wish was not granted.

If only it had been, it would have had a double benefit. Anything which obscures the Wallace monument should be welcomed. Secondly, the sooner we build replicas on the WHOLE of the country (and hand it over to Disney) the better. Because then the tourists can get Scotland as they imagine it while us natives can get on happily living a normal life without disappointed persons coming up and asking where all the kilties live.

We could all, visitors and inhabitants alike, have done with BBC Scotland's Golden Waterfall – reputedly sighted in the Campsie Hills and cascading pure whisky. This discovery was revealed on April 1st, which didn't stop some keen explorers, as the *Herald* reported, carrying empty bottles and Ordnance Survey Maps of the area in search of the magic waters.

The Worst Munro

Muriel Gray has a great deal to answer for, not least her amazingly successful programme on Munros which has possibly caused immense grief to Mountain Rescue Groups everywhere who are now obliged to spend considerable time recovering persons who, having watched the ease with which Ms Gray ascended various parts of perpendicular Scotland, think they can do the same in a pair of baffies, designer jeans and an Army surplus anorak. It is not often quite as easy at it looks in glorious technicolour. A health warning should be stamped on all of Muriel's works.

Not the Worst Monro

Beinn an Lochain suffered the ignominy of being banished from the Munro stakes. After a steward's enquiry by the pernickety surveyor from the Ordnance Survey questions were asked whether it stretched up to the required three-thousand feet. It did not.

Which makes one less mountain to climb, for which relief, much thanks.

Worst Mountaineer

Mrs Jackie Greeves who managed to get herself lost for some days in the Cairngorms. She was saved with no small difficulty and great courage from a snowy grave by the Mountain Rescue Service.

Mrs Greeves then sold her survival story to an English Newspaper for a sum thought to be £20,000.

She defended her actions by explaining that a substantial portion would be given to the Mountain Rescue Service in recognition of their work.

At the time this book was being written, no substantial amount, indeed, no amount at all had yet been received by them.

Worst Castle

There are probably more castles in Scotland than in Spain.

Not all of them are necessarily relics of Scotland's troubled and defensive past. Most notably Schloss Balmoral, that little part of the country which will be forever Coburg, set deep in the depths of Deeside. The original, perfectly respectable and even, authentic, keep was torn down by the beloved Albert who, predating Hollywood, decided that the Tower House wasn't sufficiently Scottish enough. He knocked it down to build their 'Dear Paradise'. And very dear it was too by the time Queen Victoria bought the estate for £31,500 and spent twice as much again on Albert's improvements, including enough tartan for one thousand Highland Weddings.

But there are many castles which are worse, far worse than Balmoral. Consider, at least from a tourist point of view, Dunvegan, in Skye, seat of the McLeods and home of the threadbare Faery Flag and Rory Mor's horn from which the heir to the chief must swill down a bottle and a half of claret in a one'er. It took the present chief three seconds short of two minutes. Which is approximately the same amount of time as the bossiest tour guides in Scotland (and probably GB) allow visitors to look over the whole castle. These ladies – and they are most definitely ladies – have been trained in the Stalag Luft School of charm. All they lack are the whips, the Alsatians and the jackboots. On their tours there are dungeons from which float up moans and groans, along with the sight of ghastly ghostly bodies. These are obviously tourists who didn't 'schnell, schnell' fast enough.

On an expensive little tour a little civility would be nice.

Worst Island

I passed two old men fighting one night on Glasgow's Argyle Street, under the Highlandman's Umbrella. One had the other by the throat.

'Noo apologise,' he said, 'There are so 756 islands in Japan.'

Well, it was 1990, the Year of the Culture.

Anyway I cannot remember exactly how many islands we have, but there are an awful lot of them. Many of them are uninhabited but for the sea birds, the seals, the puffins and the winds – and those tenacious tourists, the plastic flotsam and jetsam, our relics, which litter the places we do not tread in person.

There are the islands with ghosts – like St Kilda which once held thriving communities – but which are empty now.

There is a sad romance about islands which draws us in . . .

But sadder than the dead islands or even the murdered Gruinard, infected by Anthrax by the men from the War Ministry, are the lost islands.

And none is more lost than Skye which, with the completion of its bridge in 1995, has been joined to the mainland and has become an island no more – 'Over the Kyleakin Bridge' doesn't quite have much of a ring to it – excepting the ring of toll money because, at £10 plus for every return trip, it is now the most expensive as well as the ugliest bridge in Europe.

For years and years the good folk of Stroma in the Pentland Firth agitated and petitioned for a pier to be built to improve the economy and their lives. Eventually their persistent lobbying was rewarded and the pier was opened and great was the rejoicing as the first boat approached.

Unfortunately the passengers on its return trip consisted of the entire population of the island who had packed up and left at this, their first opportunity.

Worst Place for a Holiday Romance

Scotsmen and romance do not exactly go together.

Anyone seeking love should make for Edinburgh – but only in August when the Festival is on and the Capital is bung full of Englishmen and other foreigners who appreciate women almost as much as football.

The flavour of what the true Scot is looking for can possibly be gleaned from this advertisement, seen in 1995, on the back of *West World,* the community newspaper for Mallaig and the surrounding area.

'Wanted desperately by lonely Scottish Fisherman – a Wife.

Must be young and pretty. Good sense of humour. Prepared to have several children. Good, cheap, no-nonsense cook. Able to gut and prepare fish, crab and lobster for market. Must be able to saw logs, cut peat, set fires and generally run a clean and tidy home and be able to make and mend nets in spare time. Would prefer a boat owner, prefer-ably one able to be worked by one man and a boy. Please send in first instance a photo of the boat.'

Food and Drink

Worst Bar

The Oxford Bar in Edinburgh's Hill Street would be devastated if it was not given the accolade. Alas things are not quite as bad as they used to be. Its efforts, over the years, to dissuade anyone other than its few own peculiar favourite sons from standing around its cramped bar, have slackened lately. They even serve ice and lemon with the gin. They even sell gin. To

English people. But The Oxford has been surpassed by the pub in Portnahaven in Islay from which the propriatrix has removed the sign, just in case any strangers venture in. They wouldn't dare.

And then there is the pub on Harris which does not have any lampshades, only bare lightbulbs swinging in the dust, surrounded by large black-blue bottles.

However NO pub anywhere is as bad as that which serves the caravan park outside Dornoch.

It should not be missed. But then it cannot be missed on account of the large neon sign which winks from its side and proclaims it to be Grannie's Heilan' Hame in glorious technicolour. Just in case visitors dispute this claim, there is, above the bar a picture of Grannie.

Worst Gin and Tonic

The Copthorne Hotel in Aberdeen quite probably serves quite a good G and T but the twenty-five pence charged for the ice therein makes it impossible to swallow.

Worst Beer

According to the *World Beer Guide* – published in that XXXX paradise which is Australia – Scotland manages to produce the worst beer in the entire universe. There is our famed Tartan Special from Scottish and Newcastle which is dismissed as, 'fizzy, thin and pop like.' Still, they do do some awfully good TV ads.

There is also Gillespie's Draught Malt Stout whose advertisements I seem to have missed which is just as well as the book succinctly sums it up as, 'undrinkable.' I am also indebted to the Guide or its warning against Tennent Caledonian's canned Eighty Shilling Ale. Or at least its widget which, 'Gives you a four second warning before erupting over your shoes.'

Worst Meal

The Scottish diet is not one which comes recommended – except by lard manufacturers everywhere – and undertakers.

Not for nothing did we invent chips.

Or at least a Frenchman, called Edouard Déjernier did, in Dundee, where, in his chain of fish restaurants in the 1870s he introduced the chip 'finger' which was much appreciated not only by residents but by foreign seamen.

It is of course because of Monsieur D that this delicacy is now known furth of Scotland as French Fries.

Ninety years on, anything with corned beef, in Aberdeen, in the Summer of 1964, when a major outbreak of typhoid was caused by a tin of the stuff, was better avoided unless one had a burning ambition to eat one's next meal in Paradise.

I am told that those who eat at something called, if only unofficially, Salmonella Sam's, a late-night roadside caravan in Glasgow's West End, are also in grave danger.

The worst meal is any which is attempted on a MacBrayne's Ferry. No-one is quite sure whether it is the engine oil (allegedly) used in the cooking or the swell of the waves – but either way, a collation from MacBrayne is guaranteed to end up feeding the fishes.

Worst Menu Item

The Dundee Rep Restaurant always contrives to give its dishes suitable theatrical names. 'Desdemona's Delight' was not one of their more tasteful puddings, not when it consisted of two round scoops of ice-cream, chocolate ice-cream, with a chocolate flake rampant, drizzled artistically with foamy white cream. Patrons were not quite sure whether it should be reported to the Race Relations Board or the moral majority.

Worst Carry-out

Those who fondly believe that we Scots cannot see beyond fish and chips or, for the really adventurous, a curry, for the traditional Friday night carry-outs, have under-estimated the effect of travel on our taste buds.

For are we not dab hands with the chopsticks and

monosodium glutamate as well as being able to tell our Rosh from our dosh any day?

After due thought and having, as Mr Lloyd Grossman would say, caoaoaogitated and deliberrrrated between the rival claims of the deep-fried Pizza Supper and the fat pepperoni shish kebab and almost chosen the marriage between the two – that Gibson-Street-in-Glasgow-special, the deep-fried Pizza shishkebab itself, it is home-made fare which wins.

Nothing is worse than the mince pies at Hampden Park. Unless it's the Bovril at Tynecastle.

Worst Fry Up

In the Haven fish and chip shop in Stonehaven, there is a new delicacy on the menu – Mars Bar Suppers. Oh yes, for only 99p you too can enjoy chips nestling in the newspaper beside a Mars Bar deep fried in inch thick batter. But if that is a touch too strong for your stomach, they also do fried Yorkies (bars, not dogs as far as I know) and Crunchies.

Worst Scotch Broth

One of Messrs Heinz's many varieties is tinned Scotch Broth. This, according to the label proudly attached, is 'inspired by traditional English country cooking . . .'.

Worst Haggis

It would be churlish to suggest that Messrs MacSween of Edinburgh who have experimented with the national dish to make it more attractive to foreign palates could be anything other than inspired. So far they have encased haggis in filo pastry for the French, in vine leaves for Greece and put it in canelloni for the Italians.

The item on the menu of the Hong Kong Hilton during their Scottish food fortnight, described as 'A Quaich of Fried Haggis Balls,' sounds exceptional. But the worst haggis remains any haggis, especially those served at Burns' Suppers and St Andrew's Nights.

As the clerihew has it:

> One often yearns
> For the land of Burns.
> The only snag is
> The haggis.

Worst Thing in a Tin

Shortbread is a fairly harmless sort of butter biscuit but, for reasons which have never been fully explained, it cannot be bought unless first placed, mummified, entombed and encased in a tartan tin.

Worst Toast

Not that pale soggy stuff which has but briefly been hurled into a toaster and without which no 'Full Scotch Breakfast' or self-respecting Hotel and B and B, could exist, but our OTHER national toasts – those salutations, frequently sentimental or quasi-religious, said before food and drink.

'I look into your eyes and gently smell your breath.'
This is, I understand, a translation from the Gaelic.

I cannot decide whether it has lost or gained by this.
Slainthe!

Whisky

No other country has quite managed to produce Whisky as she is distilled in Scotland. That has not prevented absolutely everyone else from trying. Scotland has had a head-, not to say a hangover-start having produced the 'cratur, or something very like it for some six thousand years.

So say some archaeologists who detected spores of the stuff from 4000 B.C. on the Isle of Rhum, and they were allegedly sober at the time too.

Certainly James IV was well acquainted with it, and, by 1644 the Scottish Parliament was raising taxes on it under Cromwell. Not until the brandy trade got a pasting from the *phylloxera* vine virus in the nineteenth century did whisky begin to go on its travels and become a valuable export.

No-one seems entirely sure quite how many brands there are between the single malt Aberfeldy, and Whyte and MacKay's Special Reserve but it's an awful lot. As everyone knows, either through their taste buds or pockets, the pure malts are better than the blends and much, much more expensive.

Worst Whisky Sin

Mixing good whisky with anything other than pure water – and even that is only for big girls' blouses – is considered a terrible crime.

Except in the old mining areas where a lemonade or even Irn Bru whisky cocktail is *de rigeur*, but only with the *blends* and not the *malts* – they aren't quite that uncivilised, even in Midlothian.

In America they mix Grand Marnier with Malt and call it a 'Ritz Old Fashioned'. This practice ruins not just ONE but TWO great drinks.

However the worst whisky cocktail of them all remains the 'Harry Lauder': 1 ounce of Scotch, 1 ounce of Sweet Vermouth and a dash of sugar syrup. (Dry Vermouth and it might just be palatable but sweet . . .)

Worst-named Whisky

Naming one particular brand would be impossible – especially as your author would rather swill Listerine around her tonsils than even the best of Malts – on account of there being over 1000 different labels worldwide.

Spain's 'Dyc', I am told is well-Christened and tastes even worse than it sounds. The native Whisky Liqueur, 'Stag's Breath' from Meikle's of Newtonmore does not instil or even distil much confidence, either.

There is also 'Viski'. In the Dictionary of Russian Language this is described as, 'strong English vodka'. As the Scots

STAG'S BREATH . . .

now drink more of the Russian spirit than our own maybe
the Scotch Whisky Association should consider this as a
marketing slogan.

Tartan

Tartans breed at a faster rate than aphids on summer roses
– or even Whisky labels. By the time you have read this
there will probably have been at least another one created
by design consultants for some company or other which
has decided that all it needs to enhance its corporate PLC
(Scotland) image is its very own tartan.

From the Scottish Rugby Union to the Banks they all
want their very own mix of the ubiquitous mishmash of
multicoloured squares and stripes. Where it all began is not
entirely clear. Certainly it seems that at the beginning of the
tourist industry – when visitors came to bide-a-wee rather
than to conquer – in the early sixteenth century, tartan was
something reserved for Scottish socks or short hose rather
than a man's skirt. Quite when it became those yards of cloth
flung around the middle is not known. In fact (and whisper it
not) it seems that even tartan cloth was probably an import
from the French or Germans rather than something which
was hand crafted in the heather.

The first authenticated sighting of tartan was around
1700 when the Royal Company of Archers appeared adorned
in the stuff. As ever, the modern affliction and affection for
the more lurid plaids can be blamed on that triumvirate of
the usual suspects – Bonnie Prince Charlie, Sir Walter Scott
and Queen Victoria – who, between them, have gifted us so
much of the tatty tartanalia image which many of us could
well do without.

Some also blame James Grant, the author and distant
relative of Scott who gave the world – may God forgive him
because I am not sure that I can – the very first of the now
rampant Clan and Tartan Guides. The fact is, that when, in
1816, the Highland Society of London wrote to the Clan
Chiefs requesting that they should deposit a signed and
sealed sample of their Clan's tartan, the majority of them
hadn't a clue what it might be. Fortunately there was Wilson's
of Bannockburn, an enterprising cloth mill which produced

new patterns for its travelling salesmen every year. Now, that IS a genuine old Scottish custom which continues to this day and is carried on by the enterprising Scottish Woollen Mill chain which will invent a new ancient tartan at the drop of a loom. Or a cheque.

Worst Tartan

It is hard to choose the worst tartan, because there are so many, too many of them. But the least honourable is probably the Black Watch, known as the Government Tartan because it was in this cloth that the Regiments raised in the eighteenth century from the distressed and destitute Highlands for British Army fodder, fought and died. It is also the tartan which in its many tones is worn by the Campbell Clan. But on the grounds of taste, not to say irrelevancy, it is difficult to get past the green designer kilts created for Harrods' very own Pipe Band and their owner and proprietor Mohammed Al Fayed who not only owns the Jenners of the South but also Balmagowan House in Sutherland.

Worst Souvenirs

The best collection of the worst souvenirs can be seen at the shop in the 'Mall' at Edinburgh's Waverley Station. There are the green fluffy Loch Ness Monsters, the scotty dogs, tartan dollies, or the dishtowels with the dreadful verses, the naff postcards, miniature bagpipes and of course those sprigs of lucky white artificial heather.

All of it made in Taiwan.

No wonder then that the *Highlander*, a magazine for exiled Scots is trying to catch up. They advertise, 'Bagpipes, kilts, glengarries, Balmorals and practice chanters, all available now from: Merchandisers International, Maharajah Road, Sialkot, Pakistan.

DEER STALKING

Our Lords, Masters and Monarchs

G K Chesterton once opined that 'The clouds of pride and madness and mysterious sorrow hang more heavily on the noble houses of Scotland than on any other of the children of man', which may be pitching things a trifle strong, but which, when you examine the history of the great, if not always the good, families of Scotland is not that wide of the mark. They have been a fairly sad and sorry bunch.

What would we (and indeed this book) have done without our beloved Royal Family, or rather Families?

One Royal Scotland could have well done without is Margaret, wife to Malcolm Canmore and for reasons which escape me, Saint. She was the wretched woman who single-handedly managed to gift the Scots, or at least its upper classes, their inferiority complex. Yes, Saint Margaret, it is all down to you, this gradual anglicisation and nobbling of our nobility who came to believe that most things English are infinitely superior to anything home-grown – including accents and education. You have given us the legacy of a nation whose aristocracy, including its Clan Chiefs wear English vowels with their tailored kilts, artfully angled bonnets and steam dried eagle feathers. (Unless they are American.)

Worst Cursed Noble Family

Scotland has had its share of unlucky lineages.

Some, like the Lovats whose castle and lands have all now gone, seem doomed. Others of course are cursed.

And none more than the Seaforths.

They unfortunately fell foul of Coinneach Odhar, more usually known as the Brahan Seer, Scotland's answer to Nostradamus and who among other things foretold the coming of the Caledonian Canal, the Clearances and the North Sea Oil Boom. But he was not a man to cross.

In 1668, Lady Seaforth, wife of Kenneth Mackenzie, the third Earl, wasn't thrilled when the seer revealed things about her husband, then absent at the Court of Charles II.

She had him burned to death in a tar barrel for witchcraft but before he died he managed to croak out one last prediction – on the demise of the Seaforths. He said that the line would die, 'in extinction and sorrow. I see a chief, the last of his house, both deaf and dumb. He will father four fair sons, all of whom he will follow to the tomb. He will live careworn and die mourning knowing that the honours of his line are to be extinguished for ever and that no Mackenzies will bear rule at Brahan or Kintail.

'His possessions will be inherited by a white hooded lass from the east who will kill her sister.

As a sign that this is about to pass the deaf and dumb chief will be surrounded by four lairds: Gairloch, Chisholm, Grant and Raasay and one will be buck-toothed, one will be hare-lipped, another half-witted and the fourth a stammerer.

When the Chief looks and sees these men he will know that his sons are doomed to death and his lands shall pass to strangers and that his race will come to an end.'

It may have been a fairly long statement to make while being barbecued alive but it did all come to pass in 1815.

On a wet night it is said that the Seer still walks in Kintail and repeats it.

There were other times when it was worse to be noble.

Not least when it came to the serious crime of swearing.

In 1661 a statute was published which apportioned the penalty for expletives undeleted, 'For a yeoman: 40 shillings, for a servant: 20 shillings, for a baron: 20 merks, for a nobleman: £20 Scots.'

Although it was even worse for ministers who were fined the fifth part of their yearly stipend for the offence.

Worst Noble Family

The fact that the Campbells have been one of the most successful noble families does not make them any more likeable. It is not just that massacre, or their habit of always toadying to ruling monarchs from Robert the Bruce to Queen Victoria who, when her daughter married the Marquis of Lorne, decreed that the Dukes of Argyll shouldn't remain mere Scottish Dukes but British ones as well with a permanent seat in the House of Lords. It is not even their unerring choice of dynastic, rich brides who increased their influence and land. Plenty of others have done likewise.

There is just something deeply unlikeable about the Campbells. It sets teeth and prejudices on edge. Even the present Duke manages to irritate, because he insists publicly that he is terribly, terribly poor and can barely manage to shake a subsidy from his remaining acres. This parsimony operates at a more personal level too. Consider the poor guest who was invited by the Duke's son and heir to spend Hogmanay at Inveraray. She was thrilled. She imagined Highland Hospitality with aristocratic knobs on. Reeling, whisky and wild, wild clansmen. What she got was a single drink at midnight, followed by the click of the key in the lock of the drinks cupboard, a loud yawn from the Duke and bedtime at 12.05 a.m.

Worst Divorce

The predilection of our earliest monarchs and their noblemen to get shot of inconvenient wives, so that they could make more valuable alliances elsewhere is well known. It is a fact of blue-blooded life. Death was helpful, on account of it being about the only grounds on which a marriage could be terminated.

It was not until the more liberal divorce laws of the twentieth-century came in that our aristocracy was able to use this rather less bloody way of dispensing with a wife.

When Ian Campbell, the Eleventh Duke of Argyll decided to divorce his second wife, Margaret in 1963, it entertained the press and populace for days at a time. In a Nation more shockable then than now – and more unused to the indiscretions of its upper classes being made public instead of kept decently private – the case, with its charges and

counter-charges of sexual shenanigans momentarily riveted the country. It also puzzled them.

I mean, in those days most of us had never even heard of oral sex, far less troilism.

And then there was the mystery of the headless man. The photograph of the gent on whom Margaret had done a Gillian Taylforth. To this day his identity remains intriguingly uncertain and unproven, although some allege it was Sir Douglas Fairbanks Jnr. His father would certainly have been athletic enough. The divorce also gave us a small gem of judicial prudery from the Judge, Lord Wheatley, who said of the Duchess,

'She is highly sexed ... one whose promiscuity has extended to perversion.'

Worst Social Climber

Patricia Kluge, a former belly-dancer and married to John Kluge, one of America's richest men, was desperate to be accepted in the highest of high society. And there isn't much that is higher than the British Royals.

In her attempt to scale these Olympian social heights, Mrs Kluge first began sponsoring carriage driving at the Windsor Show.

Although she got to shake Prince Philip's paw and was even allowed to put up considerable money to fund his favourite hobby, the invitations for a cuppa' at the Castle didn't materialise.

Fortunately Mar Lodge, the estate next-door to Balmoral was on the market and Mrs K., only stopping to acquire some cashmere and kilts, prevailed upon her husband to buy it for her. The Lodge itself was extensively renovated but unfortunately, before Mrs Kluge could enjoy the delights of her Highland home or call in on her new neighbours, the marriage collapsed. And soon afterwards the house too went up in smoke after a fire. Right down the Kludgie in other words.

Worst Ghost

Scotland's Castles nearly all have ghosts. Especially those which are open to the public. Tourists like and, indeed, expect a good ghost.

No ghosts come better than that of Amelia, The Dowager Countess of Lovat, whose ghastly – and ghostly – screams, accompanied by bagpipes, haunt the Fraser seat of Beaufort Castle. Ameila's husband, the Ninth Lord Lovat, died in 1694, leaving no son but only four daughters. This was, of course, put down as entirely Amelia's fault.

But Amelia's marriage contract had ensured that if there were no male heirs then the eldest daughter would inherit.

Naturally this rather piqued her late husband's great-uncle, Thomas Fraser of Beaufort, who, but for the contract, would have got his hands on the title and its lands. So he tried to marry his son off to the eldest daughter who took one look at the future bridegroom and fled the country. Far from discouraged, the son, Simon, then set his sights on the widow Amelia. He took her prisoner and pressganged a Minister into marrying them. When she began to scream the castle down he ordered the bagpipes to be played to drown out the noise and ordered the terrified Minister to pronounce them man and wife. Then he raped her. The only good thing about this story is that Simon was eventually executed, not for the rape or abduction, but for his part in the 1745 rising.

Worst Voice

In July 1992 Lord Burton, a descendant of the Bass brewing family who owns a trifling 58,000 acres of the Highlands, bawled at a woman driving over his land. At Inverness Court he was subsequently charged with breach of the peace and found guilty and admonished.

In Court it was claimed that nurse Eileen Anderson was left cowering with fright after Lord Burton shouted at her when she stopped to allow his car to pass on Leakin Brae, a single track road.

A witness to the incident alleged that Lord B had gone absolutely berserk and accused Mrs Anderson of trespassing on his private road.

In his defence Lord Burton explained that he had always had a very loud voice and couldn't help if what he thought of as ordinary speech was interpreted by other people as shouting and screaming, 'It's just my natural tone,' he roared in Court.

Worst Drunk

It's not so much whisky and freedom which gang together as whisky and Scotland's upper classes. It's all those wine cellars I suppose. It is of course an old tradition which continues to the present day. Indeed it is rumoured that there is a special AA branch for aristos. With a whole sept devoted to the Douglas-Hamiltons.

What a pity that there was none in the 1650s when the Countess of Wemyss, Eleanour Fleming drank herself to death, aided by the doorway and stairs which she had built in her bedroom to give her direct access to her wine store.

Worst Pet

Lord Gardenstone kept a tame pig which he became so fond of that he regularly took it to bed with him.

There was also the Beast of Glamis but then no-one seems to quite know what or indeed whom it was or even if it existed. Even if the Duchess of Windsor helpfully suggested it was our beloved Queen Mother.

Lady Lucinda Mackay, the daughter of the Earl of Inchcape, seems to have had the least satisfactory pet. In Edinburgh in the 1970s she was never seen without her pet lobster which perhaps fortunately was stuffed.

Worst Tradition

Apart from the huntin', shootin', etc. our betters have this distressing habit of sending their children off to school at the age when most of them are still devoted to sucking their thumbs and sleeping with their teddies. This is bad enough. But sending them furth of Scotland for their education compounds it.

The first noble to indulge in this peculiar practice and thus gift us an aristocracy which is divorced from its own tongue and culture was Sir John Clerk of Penicuik who, in 1715 sent his son to Eton. The fact that sundry Royals were educated in the 1960s at Gordonstoun does not redress the balance, unless you really think that that school is Scottish instead of, like Balmoral itself, a little part of Germany in the Highlands.

Worst Balls

Scotland becomes part of the so-called 'season' once a year, in the Autumn, when various Torquils and Ffyonas whose blood might just once have been Scottish but which long ago got diluted by education and inclination in the South, return to their roots to reel and heuch at Private Subscription Balls.

These select gatherings (no-one but no-one gets in

without strict scrutiny of the invitation and for all I know a blue-blood test ever since the dastardly day a couple of hacks from the *Observer* gatecrashed and trashed one) in which everyone is up to their oxters in tailored tartan, are sweetly old-fashioned occasions in which archaic and complicated reels, learned solemnly in solemn evening classes in Hackney Town Hall during the Winter Months by those who don't quite know their Mrs Eglinton's Eighth from Lord John's Fifth, are danced until dawn while everyone gets hog-whimpering drunk.

The worst is on Skye. Actually there are two, on consecutive nights and both held in the Fishermen's Welfare Hall. The hall also houses the real fishermen and their guests at THEIR annual hooley, but they are not allowed a late licence on the grounds that it might encourage late drinking. The people who are so worried about the moral welfare of the lower orders and who serve on the local licensing board, are of course the same people who grant the Skye ballers theirs.

As we all know the rich don't stay rich if they chuck their dosh around – especially at the undeserving peasantry – although the pheasant are something else.

Anyway so mean are some that when a party booked in to an Oban Hotel before going off to the Subscription Ball, they enquired whether there would be a discount as they wouldn't be using the beds until 4 a.m.

The hotelier touched his forelock and agreed – so long, he explained, as they found someone else to occupy the sheets until 4 a.m. and pay the other part of the bill.

Worst Royal Meal

There are those (alright, me) who would venture that the food habitually served up at garden parties in Holyrood has few rivals in the inedibility stakes. I have it from the best sources that even *that* is not as bad as actually eating with those of the blood royal.

Guests have to stop chomping the moment their hosts do. And, as they are invariably served first this can mean doing without either pudding or coffee – or even main course as happened to many a lesser dignitary at the Queen's Grand Silver Anniversary Progress through Scotland in 1977.

The time allocated at municipal functions was short, and the guest list long, with the result that just as the meat and two veg reached those below the salt, HM would rise

and the whole delectation would be swept back into the kitchens.

But possibly the worst royal meal was the Black Dinner served up by James II to his cousins the Earl of Douglas and his brother: the final course was death when the Governor of Edinburgh Castle, Sir William Crichton ordered their murder. There was also the self-service dish given the Duke of Rothesay who, while incarcerated in Falkland Palace in 1402, to thwart, if sadly only temporarily, the plan to starve him to death, ate his own hands.

Worst Royal Mistake

To recount those errors and crass misjudgements made by our monarchs over the centuries would take not only all of this chapter and the whole book but possibly something the size of the entire *Encyclopaedia Britannica*.

From Bleary Bob, otherwise known as Robert II who had to be carried to his Coronation and who slept with anything that moved and drank everything which didn't, to Mary Stuart who reputedly did the first, if not the second, we have not been wonderfully served by our Monarchs.

Sometimes they didn't serve themselves all that well either.

James I had the sewers at Perth blocked up because he was always losing his tennis balls in them, which might have done little damage to anything other than to the monarchical nose. Except that James forgot he'd ordered the things blocked and in 1437 attempted to escape his assassins by making a smart exit through them.

Like the balls, he was trapped.

In more modern times, George IV's visit to Scotland, complete with violent plaids and kilt was not entirely wise, not least because he left two unfortunate legacies behind: his statue in Edinburgh and a precedent for royal persons to climb into what they fondly believe to be Scottish attire the minute the royal train or plane hits Caledonia. This affliction is particularly apparent in Prince Charles.

However like HRH's circumferentially-challenged forbear it does give everyone a good laugh and for that reason may be forgiven.

Along with that Cherry Brandy which the boy Charles drank on *exeat* from Gordonstoun. Anyone who rebels against that particular scholastic establishment cannot be entirely bad.

On the other hand, the *faux pas* which his mother made to receive the Honours of Scotland in her Coronation Year was less amusing. It was felt that to receive our symbols of State and Nationhood with an old suit on her back and a handbag swinging over her arm was altogether too casual.

But worse is surely HM's refusal to recognise, despite her well-logged affection for Bonnie Balmoral, if not the rest of Scotland, that up here she is not EIIR but EIR. Elizabeth Tudor never managed to reign happy and glorious over us lot even if she did sign our anointed and legitimate Queen Mary Stuart's death-warrant.

Worst Royal Remark

I suppose that about the worst thing a king or queen can say is, 'Off with his head'. Plenty of our motley crew certainly did that. No doubt plenty of them would still like to do it, especially when press persons and other vermin forget themselves and ask awkward questions.

When Prince Philip, a man not best known for his tact, addressed the Scottish Women's Institute in 1966 and declared, 'You know, British women can't cook,' I'm sure he didn't really mean to be offensive. However when the Prince, in the summer of 1995, on a visit to Oban with the Queen to open a hospital, asked local driving instructor, Robert Drummond, 'How do you keep the natives off the booze long enough to pass their tests?' it caused more than a little local difficulty. On a slow news-day the Scottish media were duly grateful for this latest outbreak of foot-in-mouth disease. This second folly in Oban did not best please those charged with promoting the town as a place of soporific

peace and tranquillity where the natives never let anything stronger than milk pass their lips.

It was the first Royal Visit to the Highland port for thirty-nine years. HM is not expected to return in the near future. There is also no truth in the rumour that Oban is about to twin with the 'slitty eyed' (copyright P. Philip 1986) citizens of Peking.

Worst Royal Marriage

The Scottish monarchs were not, I'm afraid, awfully good at marriage. Their brides or grooms tended to die young before producing a viable heir. There were only three main reasons for a monarch to marry: to secure the succession, to acquire land or wealth, and to cement alliances. Mary, Queen of Scots, only managed to achieve two of the objectives. Even those were done with different husbands. Her first, the Dauphin, gave her the alliance with France but died before he was old enough to impregnate her.

Her second, Darnley, did provide the heir but the final splicing with Earl of Bothwell lost her everything.

But when Princess Anne, the Princess Royal, plighted her troth second time around to the then Commander Tim Lawrence in 1993 in Crathie Church wearing a second-time-around-frock, it was worse.

Because, once again a Royal was caught using Scotland as a convenience. The Princess was after all confirmed and christened under the rights of the Episcopalian and Established Church of England. It was that Church which married her for the first time to Captain Mark Phillips. Which was of course the problem. The Church of England does not remarry divorced people, even Royal divorced people, without a great deal of fuss and bother and so our Church with less specific rules about such things did the needful.

Worst Royal Way to Meet a Mistress

In Royal affairs of the heart, discretion is all. It must have been easier in the days before 'phone calls could be intercepted and TV interviewers extract secrets.

Some monarchs did not even try to be discreet, including that most libidinous of men, Edward VII.

When his last and most enduring Mistress, Violet Keppel of Duntreath in Strathblane, was in residence in her Scottish home, he insisted on travelling to their trysts by Royal Train. This was not only indiscreet but also very inconvenient for other train users as their carriages were shunted (sometimes for hours) into sidings to allow their King to make his majestic way to his meetings with his paramour.

Worst Royal Meeting With a Mistress

During his even briefer reign, Edward VIII also had trouble with trains and mistresses. His worst was in the summer of 1936, when he had agreed while at Balmoral to drive over to Aberdeen to open new buildings at the Royal Infirmary. At short notice he called off his visit on the grounds that he was still in Court Mourning for his father. He sent his brother The Duke of York instead, which in itself wasn't very bright – if one brother was in mourning why not the other?

Edward compounded the offence when he was spotted

meeting Mrs Simpson off her London train. The real reason for his non-appearance became only too clear.

Worst Royal Dog

As is well known the hazards of being asked to visit with the Windsors at Balmoral are not the midges without and the Royal Parlour games within, but the corgis whose teeth fasten on any available flesh.

It is alleged that when Prince Charles' Jack Russell, 'Pooh', a present from Camilla Parker-Bowles, went missing in 1994, it was not because he got stuck down a rabbit hole but because he couldn't stand getting mugged by the Welsh mutts for a minute longer. Unfortunately the sentries and policemen whose lot it is to guard the Royals on their holidays on Deeside don't have the same option.

The latter are frequently officers from the Met. whose senior ranks supposedly use this posting as a fiendish means of punishing those of their men who have offended their superiors or who need to temporarily leave The Smoke for a cooling off period.

Worst Nickname given to the Queen Mother

When Mrs Simpson became the Duchess of Windsor on her marriage to her Duke, the exiled and abdicated Edward VIII, she was not granted the right to be called a Royal Highness. This insult she blamed entirely on the new queen rather than on her husband George VI.

From henceforth the Duchess referred to her as 'The Monster of Glamis' or 'The fat cook'. But Richard Ingrams, *soi-disant* ex-editor of *Private Eye* went further when he referred to HM as 'probably a dreadful old bag'. I am sure it was the 'probably' that hurt.

No-one has yet been as cruel to her as the Royal Marines were to her grandson Prince Edward who was known as 'Dockland Doris' and 'Babs Windsor'.

Worst Behaviour Towards Queen Mother (animate)

The fly which flew into Queen Elizabeth the Queen Mother's eye in 1947 (when she was Queen Consort to King George VI) and which delayed the Royal Train's arrival in Edinburgh by 45 minutes as (obviously) the beastie could not be removed by ordinary hands but needed the attention of a top eye consultant, qualifies as worst animate behaviour.

Worst Behaviour Towards Queen Mother (inanimate)

The fishbone which stuck in the Queen Mother's throat in 1993 when she was at Birkhall cost the BBC much overtime as they ran an overnight rehearsal of her obituary.

Worst Scottish Portrait of Any Royal

Portraits of royalty are nearly all bad if only because they nearly all look identical: at least, those of the Stuarts do. But then one man in a ruff looks much like any other. As the majority were all painted by one man, the Dutch painter Jacob de Witt, as a job lot in the 1600s, this is not surprising. He was commissioned to produce one hundred and ten portraits for the sum of £2.3s.8d., each. It took him two years. At around the same time the portrait of James VI which hung in Linlithgow Palace fell off the wall and smashed to pieces, an early example of art criticism.

Worst Loss of Royal Virginity

According to Ingrid Seward, Editor of Royal-watching mag, *Majesty*, which makes *Hello* interviews seem positively acerbic, Prince Edward lost his virginity at Balmoral (or as it is allegedly known to its staff, Immoral Balmoral) at 18 when a young housemaid crept into his single bed in his small bedroom on the Castle's first floor and did the deed.

Of course we do not know that it was the worst, but it was certainly the worst revealed and winsomely told.

Worst Royal Pilot

Prince Charles is proud of his wings, or he was, until a Royal awayday to Islay by air prematurely ended his career after a dodgy landing was made. The plane, a four-engined BAe 146, nearly crashed and killed its eleven passengers as it burst three tyres and caused approximately £1 million of damage. The Prince (now, there's a surprise) escaped all blame, even though he was the pilot at the controls, on the grounds that the Captain of the plane, Squadron Leader Graham Laurie was the real man in charge. Apparently Laurie should have wrestled the controls from the Prince and told him to get out the flight cabin. Quite.

Arts and That

As people on the BBC keep saying more people in Scotland go to museums than football matches; which is very likely true, the only problem being that many of those who go to the galleries are under the age of consent and are dragged there willingly or otherwise by their teachers and parents. We must not be churlish. There are worse places for divorced dads to take the kids on Sunday. To be both out of the rain and in an educational setting is a bonus.

Museums are the new growth-industry. They have replaced much of the old heavy industry – or rather put them in aspic with mockups of mines and shipbuilding and the rest of the detritus of our past glories. Now, there are not only the old museums full of dusty historical relics, but the new ones too. From jails to childhood, from mining to farming we've got the lot.

There is hardly an occupation left, hardly an object made anywhere, at any time in Scotland which doesn't finally come to rest in its own glass case, with its own place in its own museum.

Worst Museum

One of the places in Scotland least associated with Rob Roy (even by the American makers of the eponymous movie) is Callander. So, of course, this was the place where the local tourist board decided to pay tribute to Scotland's best-known brigand. The town is notoriously difficult to park in – thank God.

This saves some from the delights of their multimedia state-of-the-art McGregor experience, sited in a former church. It allows them instead to enjoy the other charms of a town which long-ago surrendered to the worst excesses of modern tourism, *Dr Findlay* (mark one), *et al.*

Bad though it may currently be, it was in the beginning even worse when visitors were greeted by audio information which seemed to come, thanks to the vagaries of the sound system, from the rear end of a large model cow.

Worst Exhibit

Given the number of museums and artefacts, this has not been an easy task. How can you choose between fossilized dinosaur dung in the Orkneys and the stuffed seagulls at Campbeltown?

However, having sifted through the dust and the dross, the lozenge taken from the mouth of Charles I after he got his head chopped off is truly bad. It now resides in Plockton Museum.

Not only is it totally without interest, it also lacks a certain authenticity. In its wee bit bag it looks like a '*Zube*'. And when you have seen one *Zube*, you've seen the lot.

Worst Acquisition

Joy was not unconfined when almost the entire acquisition budget for the year was lavished on 'The Three Graces' by Canova, otherwise known as 'The Three Bums'. It/they might have been better received if they had been bought outright by Timothy Clifford on behalf of National Galleries of Scotland instead of the lend-lease agreement with the Victoria and Albert Museum in London.

Three million pounds does seem a shade excessive for a visit from a statue which is rather nicely replicated by garden centres everywhere for approximately fifty-nine quid. Furthermore, because the mistresspiece is both unwieldy and unbalanced on account of those three pairs of low slung backsides, and, as marble is not the most resilient of materials, it is not expected that the statue will long survive its peripatetic life betwixt and between London and Edinburgh.

But then the whole transaction was a double whammy in some people's view because it also landed us with the aforementioned TC himself forever and ever. For the statue was secured with the help of a hefty cheque via Paul Getty Jnr whom Mr Clifford managed to offend with his remarks *anent* Mr Getty's late father, suggesting that Paul Jnr, had only contributed to spite his parent. This intemperate, if immediately retracted, outbreak of foot-in-mouth also stymied Timothy's own chances of becoming head *honcho* at the V & A. So Scotland seems stuck with its artistic *adulte terrible* for the foreseeable future – and beyond.

Worst Museum Uniform

The tartan trews favoured so frequently by the late Sir Nicholas Fairbairn QC, MP, into which Mr Clifford fitted all the male members of staff in his domain, have not been a major success although they did enliven the correspondence columns of the press for quite a considerable time. At least Sir Nicky CHOSE to dress like an American in search of his roots or his golf. The attendants are not as fortunate.

Worst Painter of things Scottish

Landseer was not as many a person, gazing on his 'Stag at Bay' over the bed in Hotel Bidawee, the worst. We have plenty who can out-MacCliché him. Including one Alfred De

HAGGIS AT BAY
by Landseer

Breanskie of whom you may not have heard but whose work has impinged on most people's eyeballs if only because his landscapes adorn (if that is the word) the public rooms and bars of practically every hotel North of the Border worth its AA rating. Indeed there are so many De Breanskies on their walls that there are those who have assumed that without him it is forbidden by the STB or possibly the planning authorities to have a hotel licence at all. He is only rivalled and surpassed by William Beattie Brown who specialises in seriously and spectacularly dull scenes of either Scottish waterfalls or mountain slopes shrouded in mist. There is always mist, but they won't be.

Worst Painting Mistake

To mark the building of the long-awaited Royal Concert Hall in Glasgow, murals were commissioned to enhance and decorate its interior at a cost of £30,000. They lasted approximately a month before being removed on the direct orders of the redoubtable Councillor Pat Lally after whom the edifice is informally and eponymously nicknamed as 'Lally's Palais'. They were replaced by some nice safe paintings which wouldn't frighten the horses or councillors.

I am told that there is also a painting by the glitziest New Glasgow Boy of them all, Stephen Campbell, bought for megadollars by an American Institution, in which a main character has three legs.

Was it meant for the Isle of Man?

Worst Exhibition

It's a toss-up really between the 1995 Glasgow *Centre for Contemporary Arts* exhibition of suicide notes and body bags brought in at vast expense from Los Angeles and the *Portfolio Gallery* contribution to the 1995 Edinburgh Festival – huge photographs of various parts of dead bodies, including such delectations as a battered head and a murdered baby's foot. Nice.

Theatre

Probably one of the worst innovations in the history of Scottish Theatre was the National Drama, a nineteenth

century invention, which gifted to the world every tat
and tartan cliché from the caricature Scotsman of Sir Archy
Macsarcasm (Richard Wilson, I do believe it, would do him
awfully well) to every kitsch and kin of the kailyard. They were
of course extremely popular. And both Sir Harry Lauder and
Rab C Nesbitt continue the tradition.

The Edinburgh Festival doesn't.

Apart from the obligatory performances of *The Thrie Estaites*
from time to time, the whole thing has very little to do with
Scotland.

These days it is really just a prolonged audition for
Channel 4 and tryouts for London Theatre.

Sadly, the prediction made by one landed Lord when
the first Festival was announced for August 12th, 1947 did
not come to pass. 'Festival?' he snorted, while burnishing
up his Purdey, 'Startin' August 12th? Ridiculous. No-one will
turn up.'

Where there's a Festival there is always a Fringe, which
in Edinburgh consists almost entirely of Drama students from
obscure American Universities and the English Regions per-
forming plays on Sylvia Plath or Karen Carpenter. Sometimes
both. Someone is always doing *Macbeth* or *Hamlet*. In 1995
there were seven *Hamlet* or *Hamlet*-related shows. And an
equal number of *Macbeths*, including one in Japanese. There
should have been a Bulgarian musical version but alas, they
cancelled at the last minute, although *Lady Macbeth Firmed
My Buttocks* did go ahead.

But the worst *Macbeth* ever was the peripatetic version
on Inchcolm, an island stuck out in the middle of the Forth.
It was in 1990. The summer was a trifle damp, i.e. chucking it
down. The audience were issued with army surplus blankets
for the crossing and the duration. I don't know if you have
ever worn a sodden wet army blanket in a thunderstorm in
August. Don't try it.

Worst Performance at the Edinburgh Festival Fringe

I haven't met anyone who actually saw the Lesbian Nude
Trapeze Artists who performed at the 1995 effort, which
leaves Richard Demarco.

But then there are those who would say that everything
at Richard's is the worst. Anyway in 1987 there was, as ever,
some company from *mittel* Europe practising its art. In the
nude. Men sat in silence, naked on the stage. Nothing much

The seats have all gone for tonight, but I can do you some wee stools by the stage –

happens until a turd slides out of one actor's anus. Much wild applause. A lady in the audience afterwards enquires on how the said actor manages to defecate exactly on cue every night – which is when Mr Demarco explains that the man had an upset stomach. And an encore or even a reprise is not expected nor particularly wanted.

In 1995 Demarco removed his entire contribution to the Festival to Dundee. It's called expanding the bounds – or something.

Worst Variety

Calum Kennedy's *Five past Eight Shows* at the Theatre Royal in Glasgow. Those who have suffered and sat through these extravaganzas assure me that a whole chapter is required but the opening number of the show which was allegedly a 'spectacular' dancing waters routine. It involved a couple of leaky wee fountains which despondently chucked up a trickle of water, occasionally.

And then there was the time Josef Locke, the singer, went on too long and had the curtain dropped on his head to stop him, not because he was bad but because Mr Kennedy was fearful that he might have to shell out on overtime.

Worst Running Gag

The comedian Walter Carr has a magnificent set of wallies. We know they are magnificent because they have been seen so often. Too often. For they have been popping out, apparently unintentionally (ho, ho, ho) for decades in everything from serious drama like Molière at the Pitlochry festival as well as every panto in which he plays.

Worst Theatrical Duo

Those furth of Scotland who have seen 'The Krankies', with the excruciating cross-dressed 'Wee Jimmy' will think that there can be no contest and no competition for the worst theatrical couple.

But they, of course, cannot match the betammied and tartanised Fran and Anna, the old pros – very old pros – of the haggis and accordion circuit.

Their act once seen is seldom forgotten.

Unfortunately.

Worst Theatrical Hoax

There are some of us who tend to think that this is anything supported by Richard Demarco at any Edinburgh Festival.

This is both untrue and unfair.

However he did play his part in introducing Anton Krashni to the public.

As did Joan Bakewell.

Mr K was written about extensively during a number of summers in the seventies when his shows were allegedly the hit and must-see of the festivals.

Unfortunately neither he nor his show existed!

Worst Critic

John Linklater of the *Herald* has the best nicknames from his rivals including 'Hannibal' and 'Mad John', on account of his renowned bad temper, and also known as GYKO (Get-Your-Kit-Off) for the way he gives ecstatic reviews for anything in which there are nubile, preferably nude, and most preferably of all *foreign* young ladies. He was once so enamoured of Tmu-Na's thighs that, in an article, he confessed to an ambition to be their sex slave.

However, the real reason he gets his award is for his rave review of a Fringe Show – written by . . . John Linklater. Modesty is an overrated virtue.

Worst Costume

Costumes are always difficult. Especially for small Scottish Companies with small budgets. The Charity Shops have dressed so many that they should be in receipt of an Arts

Council grant. But they can also come expensive. Jasper Conran has designed for Scottish Ballet. Neither was expense notably spared for Tom Stoppard's *On the Razzle* at Pitlochry. It might have been better if it had. One critic said, 'The actors dressed like oranges and acted like lemons'.

Worst Theft

Apart from the inevitable plagiarisms – and with a book like this, who am I to carp? – the worst theatrical theft was the liberation at the 1995 Edinburgh Festival of the 'Yes and No' theatre company's main prop.

The Birmingham-based group were mounting a play called *Knickers*. And it was two hundred pairs of these which were half-inched from their van.

They should try for sponsorship from Marks and Spencers.

Worst Dramatic Pretension

Many outsiders have tried to outclass us when it comes to pretensions not least at Mayfest and Edinburgh Festival times but although he is no longer resident amongst us, we have Bill Bryden late of Greenock now firmly resident in deepest Luvvie London, to outdo anything that Josef Boyes and Brecht can chuck at us.

First there was *The Ship*, the life and death of shipbuilding on the Clyde in two hours flat – very flat – in a draughty shed in Govan, followed by Bryden's best and our worst, his reworking of World War I which was so authentic that the poor bloody theatrical infantry (ie the actors) didn't get their proper recognition or reward.

They say it should all be over by Christmas –

Worst Venue

If drunk it is advisable to avoid the Traverse. Or at least to lash oneself firmly into place. Because for reasons of sentiment the seats are still more or less perpendicular as they were in the first two old Traverses.

Some of them are sponsored.

And for £75 you too can have a wee brass plate with your name on it pinned to your favourite pew – should you feel the need, a message too. I can recommend 'This is a No Farting Zone'.

'Hoping this fits your Bottom Snugly,' is much, much too twee, although just possibly in the traditions of the theatre whose first home was in a brothel.

The performers see things differently. From their point of view the worst venue ever was any variety theatre in Glasgow, particularly the Empire.

The *cognoscenti* will tell you that the Panopticon where Stan Laurel made his début was even worse – so bad indeed that the management had to cover the orchestra pit with a net to protect the musicians from the constant bombardment of tomatoes, pennies and cabbages from the audience.

Worst Spectacle

Watching the great and the good hand out lottery largess to the Arts in the very smart No. 1 Devonshire Gardens, Glasgow, (rooms £200 a night) in July 1995 should certainly be mentioned. Also, Mayfest in 1993 and all of the Edinburgh Tattoo in any year whatsoever.

None of these can surpass the three-day-long Eglinton Tournament of 1839 in which at great expense, and in grand seriousness, a whole medieval beanfeast, jousting-and-all was recreated at Kilwinning in Ayrshire by Archibald William Montgomerie, Thirteenth Earl of Eglinton.

Or at least it would have been recreated if it hadn't been rained off.

Never was such a deluge or fiasco seen, although it did provide Benjamin Disraeli with material for his endless novel, *Endymion*. But worse, because 200,000 people turned up, Eglinton devoted the rest of his life to promoting sport and encouraging ordinary people to participate in it –

and this, however indirectly, leads us to our failures in the World Cup.

Cinema and TV

In the 1990s there has been much interest in *Scotland, the Movie*. Our history has been pillaged by Hollywood's greatest with Liam Neeson turning the small red-headed nyaff and bandit, Rob Roy McGregor into 6ft 3ins of handsome, heroic manhood – *Irish* manhood. Mel Gibson does something very similar with William Wallace in *Braveheart*.

Gibson didn't, as far as one can tell, use an Irish accent and at least they put the Australian in fetching blue woad as well as the usual and unfetching tartan skirts. But Ireland had to be used as a location on account of our country not looking Scottish enough. Maybe revenge for Sean Connery as an Irish cop in *The Untouchables*? Not coming up with as much moolah as the Irish Film Board might also have had something to do with it. All of this is in the finest traditions of Hollywood.

For *Brigadoon* not even Ireland proved sufficiently Scottish or cheap enough for the moguls and they rebuilt Caledonia on the back lot recently vacated by Judy Garland for her rendezvous in St Louis. The producer, Arthur Freed, mounted a stout defence of his choice,

'I did go to Scotland' he said, 'But I found nothing there at all which looked like Scotland.' American visitors, desperately searching for heather and Highlanders in Edinburgh have been known to echo the sentiments.

We have a few moments ourselves when it comes to mugging the history on celluloid. In 1994 Bob Carruthers from Fife produced *Chasing the Deer* with Brian Blessed, financed in an altogether original way. Instead of paying the extras, the extras paid Carruthers £1000 for the privilege of appearing in the epic.

It is also in the best tradition of film and TV that all producers most sincerely believe that Scots are incapable of sounding properly Scottish. And therefore in the interests of authenticity their accents are better done by those who know exactly how Scots should really sound. The film of *Whisky Galore* did not escape the blight. And on the small screen

Dr Finlay's housekeeper in the first black and white version of his casebook was played by Irish actress, Barbara Mullen.

Readers will all have their own favourites but the worst, if only because it lasted so long on both the small and large screens, is the inimitable Engineer of the 'Starship Enterprise'– beam him up Scottie.

It is some consolation that the voice of Mickey Mouse was James MacDonald from Dundee.

Both BBC Scotland and STV have had their fair share of televisual disasters. In the 1980s, the BBC commissioned a series of late-night talk shows loosely (very loosely) based on the seven deadly sins.

It was pulled before they got past 'Envy'.

In 1993, Queen Margaret Drive also gave the great viewing public *Strathblair*, one of the dreariest, most dour and depressing series ever made.

They fondly hoped it would replace *Dr Finlay's Casebook*. It did not.

There was STV's *One O'Clock Gang* which ran at lunch-time in the 1950s and '60s and was so awful it became a cult.

It was not as clichéd as the *White Heather Club* in which large strapping lads (most of whom were moonlighting trainee gym teachers from Jordanhill) heuched on cue and danced genteel reels with equally strapping girls. Sorry – LASSIES. They were always lassies. Just as Donald always lost his trousers at least every second week.

Both lassies and laddies were taught to smile at all costs, and if you are ever fortunate enough to delve into the Beeb's archive of the shows, you can see just how much it must have cost: about 2/6 in old money.

All of these have been kept for home consumption only and have not damaged us in quite the same way as the worst TV show of them all. Arise *Rab C Nesbitt*, the programme which confirms every cliché the English ever had about drunken layabout Scots, lock, stock and string vest.

Congratulations to Ian Pattison, its author and creator.

Worst-named Programme – Ever

The Kilt is My Delight – because it bloody well isn't!

Worst Gardening Programme

In the 1970s STV decided that, to keep up with the BBC,

they too should have a gardening programme. There is not an awful lot of room for grass and things in deep-est Cowcaddens. So it was decided (and heaven forfend that anyone should suggest money played any part in this decision) that it could quite easily be based in a studio. The budget ran to a greenhouse. But not a large greenhouse. Sadly the presenter was a man whose mother must have put too much fertilizer in his milk for he had grown tall. Too tall for the said greenhouse.

But where there's a will there's a way. The problem was quickly solved by removing all the glass from that greenhouse.

No-one seemed to think it at all strange – at STV if not outwith it – that the presenter spoke to his audience with his head sticking out the unglazed roof like an overgrown petunia.

Worst Televised Hogmanay

It is of course at Hogmanay that Scotland's television stations really come into their own. If they are at all sensible these New Year extravaganzas are recorded well, well in advance of the actual event.

It may in all probability push up the bill for synthetic snow, but cuts down on the annual *angst* of worrying if any of the camerapersons will be sick into their viewfinders – again – considerably.

Live performances are, invariably, a shambles, especially when done on location and away from the safety of a nice, controllable studio with security guards and locks on the drinks cabinet.

Should all the whisky on offer be, in reality, cold tea, the enterprise is still fraught.

Today's performers are not like the troopers of old. They are used to the multiple take and retake and having to do their party pieces once in front of an audience which is either heuching or puking is unnerving to even the most professional of them.

They have all, great and small, had their disasters and forgotten not only their cues but entire songs and scripts: not to mention their exits and entrances.

Fortunately most of the viewers are usually too drunk to remember much about it the next day. But no-one has ever forgotten Robbie Coltrane's contribution to the

BBC's Hogmanay hooley which was meant to bring in, triumphantly, not only 1990, but Glasgow's year as *European City of Culture.*

The large thespian, they felt, was just the boy to do it. Sadly Mr Coltrane got so carried away with some interminable and not very funny story that, like some elephantine Cinderella, he wholly forgot about the midnight hour and spoke right through the bells, the bells . . .

And so the BBC together with the waiting world missed the first mewling and puking of 1991 altogether.

Even an empty-handed first foot might have been more welcome.

Worst Newsreader

The late John Toye although an extremely nice man, not to say an accomplished broadcaster, was just now and then known to become as tired as a newt. This did lead to some extremely interesting, indeed inspired recitations of the news, especially when he moved from Scottish Television to a brief stint with the BBC. Its brevity was not unconnected to the occasion he told the listening millions that there had been a daring break out from Safeways.

Which caused some surprise. Especially in supermarket circles, until a later bulletin and another newsreader explained that the escape had been effected from *Strangeways.*

Worst Opening of Local Radio Station

Radio Forth decided to open their very first programme with Elvis Presley. Unfortunately the disc jockey played it at the wrong speed and the late, great came out more like Tweetie Pie. But at least there was something to listen to. When Radio Clyde went on air, the microphones all went dead,

Break-out from Safeways

just as the newsreader was opening his mouth to read the first bulletin.

Scot FM did something similar. Unlike the other two, it might have been better if it had stayed silent.

Music and Pop

Scotland may not ever have been Liverpool *circa* 1960 but it has still had its successes in popular music. There have been many groups who have done their bit in the upper echelons of the charts; from *Cream* to *Capercaillie* we have played our part and sung our tunes. Unfortunately some of the things which we claim as our own were created furth of Scotland, including Mr Rod Stewart who, despite his hijacking of the tartan, Celtic and the Scottish International Football Team (as well as Irish folk tunes but that is another story for another time) was born, bred, buttered and jammed in England.

And on the slightly more elevated strata we have also had our successes what with Mary Garden, the Aberdonian who was a Diva long before Annie Lennox was thought of and Hamish MacCunn who pre-James McMillan – our most successful composer ever – gave the world both the best *and* the worst example of Scottish serious music with 'The Land of the Mountain and the Flood'. Best and worst because it was the ONLY example.

The Orkney-based English-born Sir Peter Maxwell Davies cannot count. Even if we were late starters in music on account of a certain John Knox who disapproved most profoundly of this decadent activity, by 1681 Scotland had its own worst pop group. *The Sweet Singers of Bo'ness*, a band of religious zealots who wouldn't keep their *Psalms* down and who were finally jailed to give the good citizens some peace and quiet. Eat your heart out Cliff Richard (Sir).

Worst Instrument

There are forever and always the bagpipes. Especially during the Edinburgh Festival when it is impossible to move along Princes Street without the sound of them skirling away – all of them playing entirely different and competing versions of *Scotland the Brave* and *Amazing Grace*.

Although there is no proof, it is fairly obvious that Shakespeare must have attended one of the earlier Festivals in person as well as (endlessly) in blank verse. I mean, how else would he know that, 'Others, when the bagpipe sings i' the nose, Cannot contain their urine'?

Worst Miscasting: Nearly

Many were disappointed when Marti Pellow of *Wet, Wet, Wet* didn't after all, as once mooted, play the lead in *Jesus Christ Superstar.*

If only because they were looking forward to him warbling while up on the Cross those immortal words from the Wets greatest hit, 'I feel it in my fingers, I feel it in my toes . . .'

Worst Riot

In June 1965 when the Rolling Stones appeared at the Odeon in Glasgow mass hysteria broke out in the audience and one hundred and fifty people had to be treated in hospital while another twenty were lifted by the local constabulary.

Thirty years later when *Take That!* the teenies dream group attempted something similar, but failed, two wee girls did wet their knickers but it wasn't quite the same.

Worst-dressed Group

No contest. How could anyone beat the Fran and Anna of pop, *The Bay City Rollers*? The supporters of the 1970s band maintained then (and still do) that the tartan loon pants were only a jock joke and high camp too. Maybe. Whatever, the clobber was a truly dreadful aberration, especially as they were imitated by so many with the result that for all the years of their success, it was impossible to walk down any major city without passing hundreds of wannabe lookalikes. Even M & S did a nifty line in tartan flares.

Worst Sound

It's not so much the sound of Lulu's singing voice which jars (although that could be debatable) but the one with which she speaks. Especially when she returns to the city of her birth, Glasgow, and attempts to imitate the vowels and glottal stops which she expensively lost to an elocution tutor when she decamped to fame and glory to London in the 'sixties.

But even she isn't quite as bad as Sheena Easton whose accent these days is not so much mid-Atlantic as something stuck between the Mid-Pacific and Mid-Partick.

Worst Named Band

As everyone knows nascent pop groups spend at least as much time composing their names as they do their songs. Just like their tunes they sometimes miss. Which was the case when Jim Kerr, Charlie Burchill and Charles McGraw were looking for a suitable, catchy title for their new group. I am sure that when they hit on *Johnny and the Self Abusers*, they thought they'd found the very thing. Sadly no. Jim and Charlie did slightly better with their next choice – *Simple Minds*. Unlike a certain Lanarkshire beat combo who have doggedly stuck with their original inspiration in the 1970s and are still known as *The Haemorrhoids*.

Worst-named Tour

In 1995 American supergroup *REM* had a Glasgow gig which had to be cancelled when their drummer, Bill Berry, collapsed with a brain haemorrhage.

When the band resumed touring in the Summer they tastefully rechristened it as the *Aneurysm Tour*.

Not the Worst-named Singer

The former front-man for Scottish Pop Group, *Marillion*, and now a solo performer, adopted the name 'Fish' for himself.

This may have been connected with the fact that his real name is Derek Dick. Confirmation of which can be seen in the full frontal shots he did for adult mag and boyz own comic, *Viz*.

Worst Scottish Pop Song

The problem with 'Mull of Kintyre' by Paul McCartney, is that once it is heard it is seldom forgotten. It bats between the eardrums and refuses to leave, sometimes for days at a time. It is worse than hearing the bagpipes with a hangover – worse than trying to PLAY the bagpipes with a hangover. So appallingly popular is it still, that twenty odd years after its début, it is still heard far too frequently.

Worst Reasonable Scottish Song ruined

What super Scottish Group, *Runrig* did with 'Loch Lomond' was much the same as far too many tourists do to and in the Loch itself.

Worst Scottish Song – period

'Flower of Scotland'. Would that it would wither on the kilt. It is a song well past its sing-by-date. But then, any song ever written or sung in praise of any Scottish football team, International or otherwise, is equally awful.

Architecture

It can be argued with some conviction that all the best British Architects were Scottish. From Adam onwards.

However, the Scots seem totally incapable of erecting monuments appropriate either to the person or to the event being celebrated. There are few more hideous monuments in the British Isles than the Scottish monuments. In the very heart of the country, the man who may well be one of her dearest and greatest sons, William Wallace, is commemorated by that outrageous blot on the Stirling landscape. Reverence for the man may have blinded some to the architectural defects in this unwise stone essay in overstatement. It is sometimes cited in its defence that it commands good views, true not least because it is the only place in the entire area from which there is *no* view of the Wallace Monument.

Then there are all those edifices erected to the immortal memory of Robert Burns. There is a nice irony in that just as the poet was at his most unsuccessful when he adopted the Classical verse style, he is commemorated with that Grecian temple which is the wholly inappropriate Burns Monument at Alloway. It manages to overwhelm everything in sight including real memorials to the man such as the ruined kirk, the cottage and the old brig.

It is possibly not quite as bad as the red sandstone tower tribute to him in Mauchline.

Red sandstone doesn't build well and, who, on walking down Princes Street in Edinburgh has not thought of rearranging the Scott Monument – currently on offer from the City Fathers for £1 – as something really useful such as road infill?

Which is more or less what they did in Glasgow when the city's fine, Victorian heart was ripped out to make way for motorways and bridges which go nowhere because the cash ran out before they quite managed to knock down everything built by the merchant princes and their acolytes and architects. There has always been this municipal passion for pulling down the rather good to erect the very bad.

When 'sixties city councillors took their sledgehammers to classical stone and replaced it with brutalised concrete, even in Edinburgh, the point is proved.

That Edinburgh University should collude in this vandalism by demolishing most of George Square for a particularly nasty block of high-rise offices is unforgivable. Although not as unforgivable as the capital's second worst shopping centre, the St James' Centre. The worst is the Gyle, on the western outskirts of the city. It is not only awful in itself, but causes traffic congestion of awesome proportions in an area which even before the Gyle's advent was overloaded with exhaust fumes and traffic jams.

Aberdeen and Dundee have, of course, tried to match this modernisation and are coming up fast, especially Dundee which has managed to erect its 'Discovery Centre' on a site which is well-nigh impossible to discover, set as it is in a concrete carpark, inaccessible to pedestrians.

Aberdeen has done its best to turn Union Street which was previously the finest as well as the longest shopping street in the country into a commercial death row.

Not that everything in the past was good.

Scotland's worst monument is still that weeping sore of the Clearances. Not just the Duke of Sutherland's statue, on Beinn a' Bhragaidh above Golspie, those thirty-four metres which testify to the arrogance and insensitivity of an aristocracy which laid waste a land and its peoples – but the ruined villages and settlements whose stones and ghosts still weep for the dispossessed. These are Scotland's worst, saddest, not because of any lack of artistic merit but because of what they represent and stand for.

Worst Architect

If only Sir Basil Spence had been born in the country (although Bazza does have Scottish blood) he would of course have won hands down. Or even buildings down. Which was what they had to do to his leaking, uninhabitable but (natch) award-winning Gorbals flats. They blew up the wretched things in the 1990s.

We must look elsewhere.

Now I KNOW, of course I do, that much of the work of Charles Rennie Mackintosh is a thing of beauty and a joy forever. The Glasgow School of Art, Scotland Street School, The Willow Tea Rooms, Hill House and so on. But if you have to actually sit on one of his fiendishly uncomfortable chairs for more than five minutes you think otherwise. As the said chairs are now only affordable by Lottery Winners, Museums and Banks, there is small chance of it. There are *so many* copies. Not only of his furniture but of his style. Those blasted hearts and flowers. Those wretched fronds and curlicues. That lettering.

It is everywhere. Around mirrors; on jewelry, brooches, earrings and bracelets; on clocks and watches and their faces; in Restaurants, on their menus and décor; shop fronts, particularly hairdressing salons in places as diverse as Bridge of Weir in Renfrewshire and Edinburgh's New Town, are adorned with it (quite what Toshy had to do with cuts-and-blow-dries I do not know). But thanks to him we are marooned in Mockintosh forever.

Worst Dress Designer

Scotland has not been exactly to the forefront in *couture*.

We have never recovered from Sir Walter Scott, anticipating Vivienne Westwood by a couple of hundred years and putting George IV's legs into thick knicker-pink tights for his ceremonial visit to Edinburgh.

Although we do have Nick Burns-Cumming, currently fashioning cashmere sarongs for men in pale pastels, who is doing his best. Sarongs must be marginally better than kilts.

The Written Word

Scotland of course doesn't have any literature.

Or at least not as far as the English and American literary establishments and their reference books are concerned.

All our great authors and indeed poets of the past have been hijacked by one or other. Who in England cares or knows that Byron was born an Aberdonian? But then I'm not entirely sure we want him.

Never was a poet more disliked by his contemporaries. 'The most affected of sensualists and the most pretentious of profligates' at least according to the non-sensualist and unprofligate Swinburne.

Carlyle was also taken from us by history, and by his wife Jane. According to the legend, this was just as well as it limited the damage and prevented two more people from marrying either, and also being very unhappy.

R L Stevenson, thanks not entirely to HIS wife, was early kidnapped by the Americans . . . while Conan Doyle's *Sherlock Holmes* is as English as cucumber sandwiches for afternoon tea.

Burns is anybody's.

The years have not been kind to Scottish literature in other ways.

Muriel Spark has been Anglicised – except unfortunately in the film *The Prime of Miss Jean Brodie*, where Maggie Smith attempted a tartan accent. Even when Scotland is grudgingly acknowledged, and through James Kelman wins the Booker Prize, it causes great grief and greater offence to those who think us incapable of putting one (expletive deleted) word in front of the other.

Worst Publisher

Canongate certainly, but which incarnation? Canongate Publishing (1973–90), Canongate Press (1990–94) or the current version Canongate Books (1994–?) which is of course guilty of publishing . . .

Worst Book

This.

Worst Book about Scotland

Could anything written by the marketing department of the Scottish Tourist Board which inhabits an entirely different country to the rest of us, be worse? Not much.

Although *The Unspeakable Scots*, penned at the beginning of this century by T W H Crosland, has a damned good try. Old TWH wrote the thing because he was very cross about the MacAfia which was then running the Country with three Scots (even if they didn't sound like Scots) in charge of the three major political parties: Lord Rosebery, Campbell-Bannerman and Balfour. The following quotation gives a slight flavour of the rest of this most bilious and occasionally most entertaining of works, defining the Scot as,

'. . . the fine gentleman whose father toils with a muck fork . . . He is a bandy-legged lout from Tullietudlescleugh, who, after a childhood of intimacy with the cesspool and the crablouse, and twelve months at, "the college" on moneys wrung from the diet of his family, drops his threadbare kilt and comes south to instruct the English in the arts of civilisation and in the English language.'

I don't think TWH liked us much. Even if he did have a point.

Worst Quote about the Scots

Dr Johnson, 'Sir, it is a very vile country.'
Mr S, 'Well, Sir, God made it.'
Dr Johnson, 'Certainly he did, but we must remember he did make it for Scotchmen.'

Anything Dr Johnson can say, Charles Lamb, 'I have been trying all my life to like Scotchmen and am obliged to desist from the experiment in despair' can say worse.

Neither of them quite managed to outdo Billy Connolly who once said, 'I wish I wasn't Scottish. I would rather have been born in Croatia. I don't feel Scottish.'

Worst Literary Decision

To replace the elegant and beautiful King James Version of the Bible with absolutely anything, was a mortal sin, if not against God, then certainly against the English language. But the worst of them all must be the Bible Word Publisher's of Iowa decision to produce *God's Word* which manages to translate stirring phrases like that of Mark 10, V 49, 'Be of good comfort, rise: he calleth thee' into 'Cheer up! Get Up! He's calling you.'

All of Scotland's ministers have been gifted one. I trust they know what to do with it – especially as I understand that Manses are difficult to heat and always on the look out for cheap fuel.

Worst Book Title

Book titles are frequently misleading. There is for instance a man in an anorak who is still recovering from the shock of reading Irvine Welsh's *Trainspotting*. So no doubt we should be grateful to Angus MacDiarmid for writing *The Striking and Picturesque Delineations of the Grand, Beautiful and Interesting Scenery around Loch Earn*, which is exactly that. As a bonus, it also exemplifies the worst prose; also try to get beyond its first ornate and elaborate sentence.

Worst Subject of a Gaelic Poem

I am told by those who have what they call, THE Language, that there is nothing about which a Gaelic poet will not pen a few lines: correction, many lines. Gaelic poems like Gaelic sermons and memories are not known for their brevity. But the bard who achieved ten long and eloquent verses on

Just wait till he discovers
I-Can't-Believe-it's-not-Butter!

the first appearance of margarine in the local diet takes
the laurels.

Worst Literary Hoax

Long before the *Hitler Diaries* embarrassed the *Sunday Times,*
James Macpherson, a farmer's son and schoolteacher from
Aberdeen bamboozled the literary establishment of the 1770s
with his *Poems of Ossian.* This oeuvre was allegedly a translation of the epic poems of a third-century Gaelic bard. Within
a year it had been translated into most known languages and
became in time the favourite bedtime reading of Napoleon
and Goethe.

In time, of course, these poems were also alleged to have
been found on the Führer's own bedside table and to have
influenced his beliefs.

There were – and are – those who maintain that the work
is at least in part authentic, the consensus of opinion is they
were not fragments of a forgotten culture but figments of
Macpherson's imagination.

However the real point is, if they were good – or
bad – enough to inspire both the German philosopher

Not tonight,
Josephine –

and the French Emperor, does it really matter who wrote them?

There have been far worse hoaxes, like the romantic novels of Emma Blair who was in fact six-foot-tall and very male. Worst of all, the books of the late Lillian Beckwith have fooled thousands into believing that Scotland's Highlands are indeed Toujours Auch Aye The Noo with tartan knobs on.

Worst Poet

Mr McGonagall escapes. If only because 'Claudero', James Wilson, born in Cumbernauld, when it was an old town, around 1730 did anything he could do even worse.

Like his 'Eulogy on Laying the Foundation Stone at St Bernard's Well' . . .

> 'It clears the intestines and appetite gives
> While morbific matters it quite away drives.'

Which surely beats the Silvery Tay any day. But at least neither left us the inheritance of all those appalling, sexist, drunken, sentimental, orgies known as Burns' Suppers. Anyway the ploughman deserves it. If only because he was a crashing snob who got working girls pregnant but came over all platonic, not to say Anglicised, with ladies like the excruciating Clarinda.

If he'd lived two hundred odd years later, Robert Burns would have been a natural for the *Late Show*, Melvyn Bragg's *Start the Week* and Clive James.

He would definitely have won the McVitie and very likely the Booker too.

Worst Royal Book

As *Budgie* was not written or even plagiarised in Scotland, it cannot be included. So, *The Old Man of Lochnagar*, onlie begetter, HRH Prince Charles, qualifies here. It is not so much bad, but it gives the author yet another excuse to climb into his kilt and convince the world that Scotland is still stuck *circa* 1865. When his ancestor, Queen Victoria, gave us her *Highland Journal*, it was. And they haven't televised it. Yet.

Worst Novel

The worst Scottish novel is anything written by Sir Walter

Scott . . . and the worst literary liar is anyone who says they have read, in its endless entirety, a Walter Scott novel.

Worst Translation

In this age of the Internet and all that, artificial intelligence is the thing. Edinburgh University have been working on a program which would instantly translate one language into another. They were particularly keen to do this with the more difficult languages of Eastern Europe. Long they worked, and finally fed in the phrase, 'The spirit is willing but the flesh is weak'. The machine was asked to translate it, first into Russian and then back into English again. There was a pause of only a megasecond before the machine spat out,
'The vodka is strong but the meat is rotten.'

Worst Newspaper (including worst proprietors)

The Scots read more papers than any other nationality. Proportionally its papers, not least its popular tabloids, have a higher readership than their equivalents in England. That does not mean that every paper in Scotland has been a success. The chips will never be without their wrappers so long as there are people willing to bring out such sure-fire winners as the Dundee paper which promised in 1951 common-sense news of particular interest to housewives.

There was also *Daily News*, (deceased) prop. R Maxwell – who qualifies as the worst proprietor both for his excesses on that paper and latterly of the *Record* and *Sunday Mail*. I would not of course be foolish enough to suggest that the late tycoon did anything improper to the *Record* and *Sunday Mail* pension funds; the Editor of the *Independent* found himself hauled up in front of the M'Lud for daring to caption a photo of the late Capt'n Bob with the legend that he had pilfered sundry sums. Never proven in a Court of Law, you see which means that as far as great legal minds are concerned, even although everyone else thinks it did (allegedly) happen, it didn't.

Next they'll be after the *Daily Record* journos who celebrated the first anniversary of Maxwell's swim with a special lunch – sweet course, Sticky Fingers Pudding.

An awful lot of people have tried to find the winning formula, not to mention fortune, by taking advantage of our addiction to newsprint. From Clydeside's Jimmy Reid to Glasgow Rangers boss David Murray, they have failed:

Murray's *Sunday Scot*, christened immediately, the *Sunday Scud* was very nearly the worst. Everything about it was bad, even the newsprint which seemed incapable of staying on its pages but transferred itself indelibly to its (few) readers' hands. It expired, unmourned – except by those who had thrown up their other jobs to work on it – after nine issues.

However, the very worst newspaper ever in Scotland was the *Scotswoman*, produced on International Womens' Day 1995 in place of the *Scotsman*. It was particularly hated by the female members of staff forced to work on it and who, in the name of feminine solidarity, were expected to defend something which was both paternalistic and patronising. Oddly enough the worst magazine, *Harpies and Quines*, the so-called Scottish feminist monthly tract which limply limped through 1993 and 1994 was allegedly a creation of the same person. The title was undoubtedly an extremely clever pun but the content was execrable.

Worst Newspaper Title

There are those who think that the current English dailies which put a kilt on, as we say in the trade, are the most irritating. All of them – the *Scottish Daily Mail*, the *Scottish Mirror*, the *Scottish Daily Express* and *Scotland Today*, all of which are about as Scottish as jellied eels.

However those titles are marginally less offensive, at least to modern eyes, than the weekly run by novelist Tobias Smollet in the 1760s which he called the *North Briton*. No doubt if it was still published it would be called the *Balmoral* . . . . However, if worst means 'least likely to succeed' then there is one which cannot fail. In 1976 Brian Wilson MP, perhaps mindful of his triumph with the *West Highland Free Press* or more likely that of *Private Eye*, produced a weekly political-cum-satirical magazine called *Seven Days*, which was about as long as it lasted.

This omen did not deter Jimmy Reid, from attempting something similar with his *Seven Days* in 1994. With similar results. It closed within weeks.

Worst Subject of a Column

It would be invidious to indulge in the business of chucking stones while living in the newspaper glasshouse, so the writer of the worst column will remain unnamed. But the subject of the worst column is something else. For one thing I know better than most the difficulties of finding week in, week out, *anything at all*, to write about.

We all have our old standbys and faithfuls. If all else fails there is always one's family as the *Scotsman*'s Tom Morton frequently finds out. Alan Taylor, his diminutive colleague, has an inexhaustible supply of Muriel Spark anecdotes with which to entertain us, while Jack McLean in the *Herald* can always find 750 words about his twin obsessions – drink and lassies' (as in the *White Heather Club*, they are never women but always lassies) underwear. His co-Jack on the paper, Mr Webster, will never be short of something to write about while there is still a furrow to be walked and a sigh to be sighed in memory of the Mearns.

As long as there is a holiday in the offing, critic and columnist of repute, Julie Davidson, will hitch her word processor to it.

But there are those who journey in more esoteric fields.

There was a time when that brilliant television journalist, Sheena MacDonald, wrote a column for *Scotland on Sunday*. To this day they still speak in awe of the occasion when she filled a page with a dissertation on the particular shade of yellow with which she had had her drawing room walls painted. Then there was the week when Anne Simpson, doyenne of *Herald* columnists (it is said that that paper has rather more columns than the Parthenon) wrote fluently and at length on the precise way in which French hoteliers folded their guests' pillow cases.

A relative newcomer to the trade, the former manageress of Waterstone's Bookshop, Maggie Lennon, who now edits the *Weekend Scotsman* has overtaken the lot with her piece on 'Colonic Irrigation'. A *tour de* something, if not *force*.

Worst News Editor

If Editors are absolute dictators of their print fiefdoms (and they are) the most feared and formidable satraps are their News Editors. They are not as other men or women. They thrive on death and disaster, the gorier the better. More than Count Dracula himself they crave bodies and fresh blood. It is their daily diet and without it they cannot survive.

Give them a good crash on the motorway, railway and, oh infinite joy, runway and they are happy. Reporters and photographers are dispatched and front pages held.

Great, great is their disappointment when the hacks
'phone in with the dread news
'. . . that in the pile-up on the M8 . . . on the train derailed
. . . or on board the 'plane coming down in the fog . . . *no*
lives have been lost'.

Fergie Miller ruled and ran ragged the *Daily Record*'s reporting
team in the 1970s and early 1980s.

There are many stories about his unswerving pursuit of
splashes and scoops. But his flavour is best caught by a tale
of the young reporter sent to interview a well-known and
much feared Glasgow gangster who had just been released
from an assault charge. The Jury, taking one look at his scars
and tattoos, brought a Not Proven verdict. Fergie wanted to
know how the man felt – a simple task, Fergie thought, and
one which he entrusted to a new recruit who toiled up the
many stairs of the man's high-rise to ask the question.

The young reporter was refused an answer, and when he
persisted, the 'no comment' was reinforced by an unleashing
of the thug's extremely large and equally ferocious reporter-
eating-Alsatian.

The newshound escaped with little intact, including his
dignity and, dripping blood, returned to give Fergie the
bad news.

Fergie poked him in the chest,
'Go back,' he commanded, 'The *Daily Record*,' he went on
majestically, 'Is not afraid of dugs.' It says all anyone needs
to know about Fergie to say that the hack did return without
even stopping for his anti-tetanus injection.

Worst Headline

Scottish papers are notoriously parochial. The headline in the
Dundee Courier when the Titanic sank, 'Broughty Ferry Man
Drowned' is not necessarily apocryphal.

Worst Promotion

Newspapers, as we all know, are no longer simply a means
of obtaining information. They are products, and products
must be marketed. So it came to pass that Ally McLeod,
the Scottish football team's Napoleon-at-our-Waterloo in
the World Cup in Argentina, advertised the *Record*'s new
super-duper pull-out Sports section.

There was also the TV campaign to increase the *Herald*'s

circulation which included a film of their morning conference which was almost good enough for its own soap series – possibly in Australia – especially with Arnold Kemp playing the Editor as Spencer Tracy in *Pat and Mike*. Or possibly Al Pacino in *Godfather II*. But the *Herald* when it was the *Glasgow Herald* managed an even better promotion – in 1849 it proudly proclaimed itself as, 'Scotland's least informative newspaper.'

All of them were far surpassed by the *Aberdeen Press and Journal's Supplement* to, quote, 'Celebrate the 300th Anniversary of the massacre of Glencoe', which did not go down terribly well with a Rob McDonald Parker, Director of Skye's Clan Donald Centre. It wasn't just that he didn't actually see an awful lot to celebrate about the violent killing of his forbears, it was the request that he and his Centre should *pay* to appear in said supplement which really got his blood up; plus the fact that the letter from the paper's Ad-man was signed . . . Adrian Campbell.

Worst Advertising Campaign

Everyone will have their favourites. Or not.

Like the Womens' Committee of Central Region who managed to remove the posters on their bus shelters for the movie *Disclosure* because it showed Michael Douglas's rear end.

Quite right too. It could very well have driven the passengers waiting for their number nine buses mad with lust.

The real pains are surely those jingles which keep floating around your brain for days at a time . . . Like that wretched Kwik-Fit Fitter.

If they had confined it to TV it might have been bearable, but every time it was seen on a hoarding, the tune immediately began its refrain in the head.

Sadly NOT the Worst Advertising Campaign

When the Durex Company were looking for a new and original way to publicise their product they thought they'd cracked it when one of their executives rode one day on the Clockwork Orange, Glasgow's idiosyncratic Underground system. The shape, as it were, reminded him of something.

And so it was that they applied to Strathclyde Transport Executive for permission to sheath a train in a giant condom.

They were willing to pay £1 million.

It was a lot of money.

But then the Executive remembered that their train went through Kelvinside and reluctantly decided against it.

The Law

Although there are many who choose to forget it, including most in Westminster, the London media and BBC's John Birt, Scotland has its own judicial system. There are those who might argue otherwise, but it could be said that Scottish Justice has, on the whole, served us well.

There have been notorious miscarriages of justice, including the Paddy Meehan murder case, but our courts have, largely, escaped some of the worst excesses of that legal system to the south of us. We are proud to preserve our share of eccentrics and eccentric verdicts. In Scotland, after all, it is still an offence to be 'Lewd and Promiscuous'. No-one has ever quite got round to repealing that aged statute. It is quite some time since the due sentence or punishment has been carried out:

'That the offender be taken to the foulest and deepest pond within the Parish and ducked for no more than ten minutes.'

One is glad, too, that the late, great but also lewd and promiscuous Sir Nicholas Fairbairn, QC MP, wearer of the worst wardrobe of clothes known to any Scot within or without his profession, was never charged with the crime, if only because it would have played havoc with his pale linen Nehru jackets and Gordon-tartan trews.

There were some other good old laws too.

In the fifteenth-century Scots were forbidden, on pain of death, to marry English women without express permission of the King – which was seldom given. I do not know if it was O.K. for Scotswomen to marry Englishmen.

Worst Result in the Appeal Court

Members of the Faculty of Advocates have an institution known as the Hole in the Head Club. This august body is made up of that happy band of lawyers who have managed, on appeal, to *increase* their client's sentence. Included in their number are Leona Dorrian QC who managed to get a six year stretch upped to ten, and Ian Duguid who didn't do at all well when his plea earned his man a trebling-and-more of the original sentence from nine months to thirty months. Mr Duguid was particularly irritated because he had previously thought his client dead lucky to get less than a year and had wanted, nay begged him, not to appeal.

Worst Heists

On the Isle of Bute two desperadoes attempted to rob the local bank. Unfortunately, it had a revolving door in which one of the robbers got caught on entry to the building.

He was rescued by a staff member. Ungratefully, he then pulled a gun and demanded £5000 from the young female teller. He explained that he needed it to go round the world. He invited her to accompany him but she refused both him and the £5000. So he asked for £500 to get him to London instead, and when she still wouldn't he dropped the price to 50p. When that was not forthcoming he said he would shoot her. 'Go ahead,' she shrugged.

Meanwhile his companion managed to grab £600 but, sadly, on their way out they pushed the revolving door the wrong way and were both caught.

There was also the Glasgow thief who stole £2000 from a bank in Milngavie and escaped on a bike. As he was completely bloottered at the time, he fell off. Two workmen helped him back on and were given £200 each. After their full description – and full refund of the money – the man was arrested in a pub. The bike was propped against the door.

Worst Judge

Naturally, and having read my Scots Law on Judge-Murmuring, I recognise that all the men (there are no women) currently adorning the Scottish Bench are all possessed of huge integrity and dispense justice as wisely and as well as Solomon. Naturally. Some of their predecessors have been less distinguished.

Robert MacQueen, Lord Braxfield, is known as The Hanging Judge for fairly obvious reasons. When the radical Joseph Gerrald was tried before him for sedition, he ventured to point out to Braxfield that Jesus Christ too had been a reformer. Braxfield scratched his wig

'Ah weel,' he said, unimpressed, 'Muckle He made o' that. He was still hangit.'

There was also Lord Miller of Barskimming – which when you consider it, might be the worst name for a Judge. He had a longstanding feud with James Boswell, an Advocate for longer than ever he was Dr Johnson's cheerleader. And like all Advocates Boswell hated to lose a case. But none upset him more than when his client John Reid was accused and found guilty of sheep-stealing in 1774.

Lord Miller put on the black cap and sentenced Reid to death.

Boswell fought long and hard to save his client, and when all appeals to higher authority failed, Boswell planned to have Reid cut down from the West Bow scaffold and resuscitated. Unfortunately – for Reid at least – Boswell was dissuaded and the man died but until the day Boswell did the same he railed against both judge and verdict.

Worst Fraud by Lawyer

There are those who think that the whole judicial system is a fraud.

There are those lawyers who think the whole system is there to be defrauded. Many and notorious have been the cases in recent years. None have surpassed Edinburgh solicitor, John McCabe, who in 1991 was found guilty of thirty-five separate charges of dishonesty. Over seven years he managed to liberate sums totalling £4.3 million, mostly through property fraud. All the money was repaid by the Law Society of Scotland's guarantee fund.

Worst Fraud by Non-Lawyer

In the late 1980s a quiet, self-effacing accountant called Williams came to live at weekends and holidays in the delightful Highland village of Tomintoul. It was obvious that he was a man of some substance. At first he kept himself to himself and nobody was quite sure what part he played in the financial affairs of the nation but it was obviously something very important – and well paid – which made him commute to London every week. He bought himself and his lady a fine country residence on which no expense was spared and then began buying up various properties in the village. In particular he acquired a run-down 'grand' hotel, a relic of the optimism of another era and financed its much-needed refurbishment on a suitably generous scale. It slowly emerged that he was a Lord, the scion of an ancient Borders family and, not surprisingly, he soon became known to the locals and visitors as the Laird of Tomintoul.

The Laird of Tomintoul was much respected, even more so as he spread his money about and brought prosperity and jobs to the village. It was only when the Metropolitan Police did an audit and discovered sundry monies missing from the funds used to bribe narks and rehouse high profile witnesses, that it was realised 'Lord' Williams was in fact a rather badly paid accountant with the Met., who had 'redistributed' the money in his adopted Lairdship.

The local population still remember him with affection – oh aye – the hotel is still open and indeed, said to be flourishing.

Worst Judicial Opinion

When James Boswell and Dr Johnson were on their Scottish Tour, they went out of their way to visit the Court presided over by the learned but eccentric Lord Monboddo. Watching him at work was a recognised entertainment for important tourists and visitors.

Born James Burnett in 1714 and called to the Bar in 1737 Monboddo was also a leading mover and shaker in the Scottish Enlightenment. Apart from dispensing the Law, his particular interest was in the origin of man. Before Darwin, he maintained we were all descended from the orang-utan. He felt that we all still had tails which, because of all the sitting down we indulged in, had elongated and flattened into buttocks. Dr Johnson was not convinced!

Worst Mistake at the Scene of a Crime

When the SS *Politician* (of 'Whisky Galore' fame) sank off Eriskay with 20,000 cases of whisky on board, there were many unofficial salvage attempts. The local schoolmaster sought permission from the local Home Guard Commander to save the ship's piano (shurely some mishtake?).

Worst Mistaken Identity

As someone once said England (and TV) may have Rumpole of the Bailey, but we've got Beltrami of Barlinnie.

Or rather those who have been accused of committing heinous crimes and don't fancy a holiday at HM's pleasure in the Bar L. have the Glasgow solicitor/advocate, Joseph Beltrami.

Anyway Joe has a no doubt deserved reputation among the criminal classes as a good man to have on your side in a bad case.

He has become a legend, as they say, in his own lifetime.

Even if his grasp of other legends is not quite as high.

For it came to pass one day that Joe, about to make his plea in mitigation of a client ran from Court, buttonholed another lawyer and said, 'Quick, name me that mythical beast which rose from the dead.'

And so it came to pass that the legal eagle returned, 'My Lord,' he pled, 'this man has suffered much family and personal grief but he has overcome them and risen like a salamander from the ashes of his life.'

Worst Legal Insult

When Sheriff Rosie Morrison was an advocate she did a stint abroad. In Hong Kong to be exact where the female silk's charms were no less appreciated than they are in Edinburgh drawing rooms and the country's Courts.

Unfortunately some or rather two of Ms Morrison's charms proved a little too much for an opponent on her sojourn abroad who complained that he couldn't concentrate on his case because he could see the lady's breasts under her blouse. Rosie was suitably scornful.

As she said, the time she would start worrying about her chest would be when it could be seen through her tights.

Worst Animal Behaviour in Court

When six men were charged with Terrorist Offences at Falkirk Sheriff Court in August 1995, security was very tight.

The Court was guarded by trained marksmen while Strathclyde Police brought in their sniffer dogs to make sure there were no explosives secreted anywhere. Tension rose as the team's crack mutt, a black Labrador, began to work overtime. Great sniffings and barkings ensued.

Evacuation of the building and the advent of the bomb squad seemed imminent. until the Court Officer, Alex Stormonth fumed,

'That bloody dug's eaten my piece.'

But 'George' and 'King', Shire stallions, did worse. In November 1994, farmer Jimmy Wilson from Kenmuir Farm at Mount Vernon, near Glasgow, brought two horses into

Glasgow Sheriff Court as principal witnesses in a Civil action. They got through the plate glass doors alright but were then slung out, not without leaving the evidence of their short stay behind.

In August 1995 Mr Wilson was charged with allowing his horses to foul the foyer.

He was found guilty and fined £450.

He paid up reluctantly pointing out in mitigation and quite reasonably that,
'There are no such things as nappies for horses.'

Worst Treason Trial

If it had taken place in Edinburgh rather than in London, the arraignment and conviction of William Wallace on the charge of treason would easily have been the worse injustice ever recorded. But as the foul deed was done outwith the jurisdiction of this book we must settle instead on the trial of the Cathcart Commandos in the 1970s.

This gang of desperadoes was rounded up by the Special Branch who were convinced that they had rooted out a dangerous bunch of extreme nationalists, on a par with the Provisional IRA who were about to bomb and blast Scotland into a fight for independence. Alas as the case wore on it became clear that the Commandos were, in truth, a folk group and all their followers were not fanatics willing to fight and die for the cause but fans who liked their music.

The case was dismissed with much scrambled yokes on police persons' faces.

Worst Civil Dispute

The best advice – and the cheapest – ever given by any lawyer is either to forget the perceived wrong or to settle out of Court. In spite of this, sundry persons continue to hire lawyers and to merrily sue neighbours and relatives and erstwhile friends.

Husbands have fought with estranged wives over the custody of pets. Ex-wives have disputed the ownership of wedding presents with former husbands – which neither liked nor wanted while married. Neighbours have gone to war over the parking of cars, the barking of dogs, the placement of hedges and fences and the incursions of cats.

But only the Earl of Tweed in 1692 ever claimed the carcass of a whale and went to Court against one William

Erskine who had found it washed up at North Queensferry on the River Forth. The Earl lost.

Worst Family

When God made Scotland it is alleged that He said to Gabriel, 'I have created this wonderful land. It has magnificent mountains, glorious lochs, rivers full of leaping salmon, fields waving with grain and its scenery would take your breath away.' And the Archangel remonstrated with the Lord and said, 'Surely it is wrong to give so many marvellous things to one country?'

And God replied, 'Ah, wait until you meet their neighbours.'

Anyway in 1995 the legal profession – and the press – found a whole new area of criminal behaviour – the so-called Families from Hell who put their neighbours in fear and trembling.

Although many aspired to the title, including 17-stone Mags Haney from Raploch in Stirling and her brood who had over 300 court appearances between them, by common consent the first, the Grahams, late of Glenrothes whose children and dogs terrorised their entire neighbourhood, deserved it most.

Their idea of neighbourliness included chopping down a telephone pole and knocking out all the lines in the streets, rigging up floodlights from the street lamps and pelting neighbours who complained with excrement and eggs.

The local bus company rerouted their vehicles rather than allow them to face the regular ambushes from the younger Grahams and the binmen were too traumatised by a combination of Rottweilers and thrown bricks to empty their rubbish.

When they finally left – after propping a Saab against the front door to stop the bailiffs from evicting them – it was like VE day with street parties, dancing and general rejoicing all round.

Worst Cop

When there is a big football match pending, it is not unusual for Transport Police to travel on the trains to quell the fans' high spirits. They will sometimes board coaches en route if complaints are made by other passengers or the conductor.

In September 1995 when an InterCity express stopped

at Darlington on its journey south from Scotland, the police piled on after being alerted to the mayhem caused by supporters on their way to a match in Norwich.

The only slight problem was that the game was the Transport Police's own tournament.

And the fans creating the trouble were all off-duty members of the force.

Worst Excuse for a Bullet-Hole

When the later Arthur Thomson, the so-called Glasgow Godfather (whose son had already been murdered by rival gangland operators in 1991) was taken to Casualty with bullet-wounds, he maintained he had suffered the injury by getting run over by a car.

Worst Excuse for Carrying a Gun

Glasgow Sheriff Court: the Lawyer was young; his client was charged with recklessly discharging an air-pistol in a public place. The fledgling legal chick was in full flow explaining that the gun was used only for hunting. The Bench was moved to enquire exactly what it was that the accused hunted in the Glasgow area. The Lawyer knew the answer,

'My client uses the gun to hunt slugs, your honour,' he said confidently.

Well indeed, I mean whatever else would you use a slug gun for?

Worst Modern Mass Murderer

Scotland has not had many serial killers – at least not in modern times. Historically we have had our share – and then some, from Macbeth to Butcher Cumberland. But in the 1950s there was Peter Manuel who was found guilty of seven murders and was suspected of carrying out considerably more.

He was hanged in 1958, probably the nearest we have managed yet to a Peter Sutcliffe or a Fred West.

But although Manuel was, without doubt, evil, there is something particularly repulsive about child murder.

There can be few worst than vanman Robert Black from Aberdeen who killed Susan Maxwell in the Borders, Caroline Hogg at Portobello and at least three other little girls in England, over a ten year period until he was finally caught while in the act of another abduction. He is currently serving ten separate life sentences in an English prison, and at least ten other police forces are currently considering questioning him about the deaths of other children.

Worst Modern Mass Murderer (undetected)

In the 1960's Glasgow's female population went in fear of 'Bible John'; so-called because, according to a witness who shared a taxi with him and who was a survivor of one of his attacks, he extensively quoted scripture. He was thought to have been responsible for three murders. All the women he killed were picked up at *Barrowland*, the Glasgow Dance Hall. Despite a full and detailed description of him, he was never caught. Unlike other serial killers, for some reason, Bible John stopped his murderous career almost as suddenly as it began.

Worst Reason for Divorce

In 1972 a wife sought a divorce in the Edinburgh Courts on the grounds of cruelty. Her husband, she explained was always coming home very late at night. This, she explained was not the cruelty of which she complained – but it caused it because when he finally joined her in the matrimonial bed, his feet were freezing cold and he warmed them by putting them on her back. The divorce was granted.

Worst Crime

Rural Scots have long resented the rest of Scotland's questioning of their choice of sexual partners – in other words, sheep. In July 1995 there was evidence that yet again the townies had got their country cousins wrong – when a seventeen-year-old from Tranent in Lothian was charged with committing sex with a HORSE.

My apologies to the slandered sheep.

Worst Jail Sentence

Several Salvation Army Officers, in 1882, were sentenced to imprisonment for the heinous crime of leading a March on the Sabbath.

Worst Mistake Made by a Judge – Outwith his Court

One winter morning in the early 1970's, Lord Stott stopped to help two nurses who were stranded in thick fog on the side of the road. His Lordship gave them a lift. As they left his car, his lordship said that should he ever end up in their ward, he hoped they would look after him well. The nurses assured him that not only would they look after him well but they would make a fortune as they were both midwives.

Worst Mistake by a Lawyer in Court

It was January, a time when, in the Courts (as elsewhere) men and women show off the presents gifted to them in their stockings by their loved ones. This is more difficult for advocates and lawyers who must abide by a strict dress code. A lawyer's wife, anxious to please her husband (but not to displease the Justiciary) gave him that most intimate of tokens, new underpants, but underpants with a difference. Thus it was that the Court listened, in the midst of the lawyer's impassioned plea for his client, to the sound of Jingle Bells, tinkling out of his nether regions.

♫ Oh what fun it is to... ♫

Worst Plea in Mitigation

When a Glasgow working girl was up before Baillie Bill Aitken in the District Court, she was fined the usual £100 – with time to pay at the usual rate ten quid per week.

'Haw, gie's a break,' she said, 'I cannae pay that much.'

The Baillie asked why not?

'It's ma back,' the professional replied, 'I've hurt it and it's fair killing me.'

Mr Aitken instantly understood that a back was a tool of her trade and extended the time to pay to three pounds weekly.

Some clients are less lucky. Like the man defending himself on a 'Breach of the Peace' charge at Falkirk Sheriff Court. He was found guilty and asked if he had anything to say in mitigation before being sentenced. He thought for a moment and said,

'Aye. I suppose I'm just an erse.'

Worst Court

During the refurbishment of Paisley Sheriff Court in 1995, temporary quarters were found in a defunct school. This establishment unfortunately was on the edge of the town and far, far away from the necessary legal support systems, i.e. decent pubs and restaurants. Space was also very limited and the authorities told the lawyers that they had room for either a legal library or a billiard table but not both. The billiard table has been a huge success.

Worst Excuse for Murder

In Paisley in the 1980's a man accused of murdering his brother was asked why he did it.

The man was in no doubt that he had a due and just cause, 'He ate ma pie,' he explained.

Worst Fairbairn Story

The anecdotes about the late Nicholas Fairbairn QC MP's behaviour are as many and varied as his eccentric wardrobe. But then both were chosen to shock and possibly to amuse.

Although even those on his own side, including friends, were taken aback when he opined in 1994 that there was really no such crime as rape.

But by then his beloved drink was controlling his tongue as well as his liver. And it was of course booze which generally led to many of Nicky's more eccentric exploits.

Including the occasion on which he was asked to dine at the Belgian Consulate. For some reason he took against the Consul and all his works, not least the food and drink provided.

He was, as an honoured guest requested to taste the wine.

This Fairbairn did, rolling the liquid round his mouth in the requisite fashion – before spitting it out, just missing his host's wife but not the beautiful snow-white damask table cloth.

When it was suggested to Nicky that an apology was due, he immediately agreed. As he said anyone who served a vile wine like that had a great deal for which to apologise.

Worst Question in Court

Neil Murray QC was doing his stuff in Edinburgh's High Court. The witness he was cross examining was a prostitute.

'So,' Mr Murray asked, 'does your work involve close contact with men?'

Worst Sheriff (motoring)

Sir Steven Young of Greenock is not a man to treat lightly those who turn the breathaliser red, jump the amber or who exceed the speed limit. As for drinking and driving, dire warnings should be posted at the entrance to Sir Steven's

territory. Even wine gums could get you banned. There are those who think the only way to negotiate the roads in his fiefdom safely is to travel in convoy at three miles-an-hour with a man carrying a red flag walking ahead. But Sir Steven would have them for obstruction.

THE COLD WITHIN

Six humans trapped in happenstance
In dark and bitter cold,
Each one possessed a stick of wood,
Or so the story's told.
Their dying fire in need of logs
The first woman held hers back,
For of the faces around the fire,
She noticed one was black.
The next man looking across the way
Saw not one of his church,
And couldn't bring himself to give
The fire his stick of birch.
The third one sat in tattered clothes
He gave his coat a hitch,
Why should his log be put to use,
To warm the idle rich?
The rich man just sat back and thought

Of the wealth he had in store,
And how to keep what he had earned,
From the lazy, shiftless poor.
The black man's face bespoke revenge
As the fire passed from sight,
For all he saw in his stick of wood
Was a chance to spite the white.
The last man of this forlorn group
Did naught except for gain,
Giving only to those who gave,
Was how he played the game.
The logs held tight in death's still hands
Was proof of human sin,
They didn't die from the cold without,
They died from the cold within.

Politics

Someone once said that if there were only three Scots left in this country there would still have to be four political parties to accommodate them. This might very well be too few.

In the Perth and Kinross by-election of 1995 there were nine different parties, from Tory to the now almost obligatory candidate from the Raving Loonies. This political plethora is not a modern phenomenon. In the Glasgow local elections of 1932 the Moderates, Labour, the ILP (Independent Labour Party), Communists, Scottish Protestant League, Scottish Nationalists, and Independents were all represented. Whether this interest in politics is because of or in spite of not having our own parliament remains a moot point.

Whatever the case, politics in Scotland has always been a robust game. Gladstone and, later, Winston Churchill were not the only politicians to face the wrath of their unruly electorate. The Baroness herself, M'Lady Thatcher, was confronted by a man who threw paint at her outside her Glasgow hotel.

Worst Accent from a Scottish Politician

Michael Forsyth, the Scottish Secretary, may be a Red Lichtie, in other words, born and bred in Arbroath, but he has certainly buttered his current mellifluous tones in a gentler place.

Robin Cook MP is politically very far from Forsyth. Yet, since he has edged ever closer to power his accent too has been polished and honed into something altogether much grander. Perhaps New Labour is not only filching policies from the Conservative Party, but its elocution teachers too. But at least both sound as recognisably coming from somewhere which is approximately Scotland, unlike Foreign Secretary, Malcolm Rifkind, whose poshy peculiar accent bears no resemblance to anything remotely this side of Hadrian's Wall – or indeed remotely this side of anywhere. One fears that Mr Rifkind may fondly believe that he has purloined it straight from Eton, or perhaps from his predecessor and real Etonian, Douglas Hurd.

Worst Name

When will Peerie Norrie from Shetland ever learn to accept that his fine old name is pronounced as LamonT and not La Mont, not matter what his pretensions? Incidentally, did you know that his maternal grandfather, Charles Hughson, once lived in a croft called 'Loot'?

Worst Affair

The Honourable Members, male and female do seem to have had terribly bad luck in their affairs of the heart, i.e. they keep getting found out. They managed these things altogether better in the days of Harold MacMillan whose wife, Lady Dorothy, enjoyed a long liaison with Lord Boothby, including having a child by him which the saintly Mac accepted. But that was of course pre-telephone, fax and tabloid.

It is much more difficult now. Especially, for instance, when one's former girlfriend tries to hang herself on a lamp-post outside one's flat, as happened to the late Sir Nicholas Fairbairn.

George Galloway, Hillhead's finest, did not do himself an awful lot of good either when he confessed in an interview that he had had carnal knowledge of a female chum on an overseas spree – sorry, important fact-finding mission.

Former Labour MP for Leith, Ron Brown, ended up in Court after a very public fracas with his mistress over a pair of knickers.

But the worst affair was that which Winifred Ewing SNP MEP alleged had taken place in the 1970's between Roseanna Cunningham, now an MP, but then a lowly assistant at the Nats' Edinburgh HQ, and her boss, one Donald Bain.

At the time of the relationship Mr Bain was married, although officially separated from his MP wife Margaret.

In time Margaret Bain, divorced, lost her seat, took Mrs Ewing's son as her second husband as well as winning a new Constituency and everyone should have lived happily ever after. Except that twenty years on, in 1995 when Ms Cunningham sought selection as the SNP's candidate in the Perth and Kinross by-election, Mrs Ewing Snr attempted to stymie Roseanna's chances by dredging up the old non-scandal with Donald Bain.

She failed.

But succeeded in tarnishing her own distinguished career and reputation.

Worst Secretary of State for Scotland

The Duke of Richmond who held the post for a year in 1885 and never quite managed to cross the border. There are those however, who wish the present Scottish Secretary would do likewise.

Worst Political Conversion

A Young Conservative some twenty years ago presented a paper to his elders on the necessity for Devolution and a Scottish Parliament. His name was Michael Forsyth. Five years after that, a Labour MP called Brian Wilson was sitting on platforms with presidents of the CBI and other establishment grandees explaining exactly why Devolution was a bad thing.

Worst Sexism

The new Convention for a Scottish Assembly, an organisation dedicated as much to political correctness as a Parliament for Scotland had just finished a very successful meeting. Labour's Harry Ewing was giving the vote of thanks,
'I want to thank all of you for coming here today – and a special word of appreciation goes to the lassies who typed the papers and made the teas for us.'

Worst Political Prediction

Predicting the future is something at which politicians are rather less successful than Mystic Meg. There has never been a candidate yet, not least at by-elections, who has not become especially prone to hyperbole and who has not ringingly declared that he or she expects to be collecting a

Go back to your Constituencies and prepare for Government!

pay packet from Westminster soonest. And all the Parties are prone to exaggerate or misread the runes and the opinion polls. As the electorate never takes a blind bit of notice it hardly matters. And yet I think most of us remember, thanks to telly, Sir David Steel exhorting his troops to, 'Go back to your constituencies and prepare for government!'

Whilst the SNP's Alex Salmond might wish that that catchy phrase, 'Free by '93' had never left his lips.

Back in 1922, Sir John Cargill, in a speech in Glasgow, forecast that the Labour Party was just a passing phase. Fair do's. There was a time in the 1980s when it seemed it might very well come true. But the People's Party has kept its grip on Scotland. Scotland keeps its grip on them too with the result that they are always anxious about getting home from the Commons for the weekend. One Thursday evening, fog was forecast for Scotland and some MPs were undecided about whether they should make immediately for Heathrow or settle instead for the overnight sleeper. Fortunately, Tommy Graham, the MP for Renfrew West and Inverclyde has his house at Linwood, only a runway away from Glasgow Airport. Graham rang his wife and asked her to stick her head out the kitchen window to see if all was well and planes were landing. After a suitable interval, she confirmed that visibility was fine and Graham passed the good news to his colleagues. It was however quickly pointed out that some of them were flying to Edinburgh, 'Nae bother', said Tommy, 'I'll just give the wife a bell back and ask her to run upstairs and have a look from up there.'

Worst Romantic MP

As we all know, especially if we read the *News of the World*, our MPs manage to have more romantic encounters than most of us. Indeed the author was once sent by an Editor to see how long it took to get picked up in the House's Central Lobby. Two minutes. Of course that was in another country and besides the wench was younger then. But some MPs are made of sterner stuff, including Donald Dewar, the Most Honourable Labour member for Glasgow Garscadden. While fixing a meeting of the Scottish Constitutional Convention with colleagues, St Valentine's day was suggested. 'When's that?' inquired Mr Dewar.

Worst Election Leaflet

They are all pretty dire, but John Corrie, the Tory hopeful for Argyll in the 1992 General Election, was worse than that. He informed an awestruck electorate that he had once clipped two hundred and twenty-one sheep in nine hours to secure the Scottish Shearing Championship. But just in case that wasn't a clincher, he capped it with the information that, 'In 1979 I was awarded the Wilberforce Plague for Humanitarian Work'.

He wasn't awarded the seat. And even it had been the Wilberforce *Plaque*, would he have fared much better?

Worst Political Prediction by a Newspaper

On the Sunday before the Govan by-election in 1987, the *Sunday Mail* confidently stated: 'If there is one thing certain it is that a Labour Member will be returned next Thursday.'

Worst Result

When the late William George Boaks – Public Safety Democratic Monarchist White Resident as it said on the polling paper – stood in the Hillhead by-election he received five votes, probably from one Democrat, one monarchist, one white, one resident and a man with a bike.

Worst Word

It could be argued that the hard-fought Govan by-election

of 1987 was won for the SNP's Jim Sillars by a single word – 'additionality'.

Because it was his political opponent, Trade Union official and Labour Party hopeful, John Gillespie's inability to understand it which allegedly tipped the votes Sillar's way.

Not that many people did exactly comprehend this piece of EU-speak which is the means by which every pound given from Brussels for development projects is supposed to be matched by an equal amount from the British Treasury. I think. Anyway all the candidates were taking part in a televised debate during the campaign and the first question put was on this complicated matter.

Mr Gillespie was visibly left floundering to delight all round. Especially Jim Sillars who leapt in and made political hay with his major rival's inability to finesse past the subject.

Collapse of morale and Labour's campaign all round.

Not least because Gillespie was constantly harassed and heckled on it *ad infinitum* – no doubt unfairly by the political hacks and jackals who themselves hadn't previously a clue about the meaning of 'additionality' themselves. As they said, they knew old John couldn't string two words together, but you might have thought he could have managed one.

There was a postscript to this event.

At the next Scottish Labour Party Conference, Gillespie rounded on a couple of his journalist tormentors, 'See you,' he said, stabbing an accusatory digit at them, 'That word doesn't exist. I know because when I got home I looked it up in my dictionary and it wasn't there!'

The journalists weren't quite sure whether he wanted to sue the publishers or demand that the contest be rerun.

It was also in that by-election that Mick McGahey, then of the Miners' Union, was out supporting the Communist candidate, Dougie Chambers.

He was interviewed by a BBC luvvie from London and waxed long and eloquently about Dougie's hopes and plans for the constituency.

The interviewer, a very superior young lady from the Paxman school of charm, interrupted Mick in full flow with a scornful, 'Come on, be serious, you can't really expect him to win.'

McGahey breathed heavily into the mike and in his unmistakable basso profondo said, 'I have to admit that at this point in time, Govan is not yet a safe seat for the Communist Party.'

Worst Political Programme

Kirsty Wark is of course now universally recognised as one of the country's foremost and best broadcasters. But in 1985 she was co-presenter of something from BBC Scotland called *Right, Left and Centre*. The programme went out live on Friday nights straight from the most uncomfortable set ever devised by the design police. Ms Wark and her guests crushed – or tried to – onto a green bench all of six inches wide, to which they desperately clung as they attempted to discuss Scotland's political future. The fun for viewers was rather more immediate – would anyone fall off before the end of the interview? Especially as Kirsty's co-presenter was one Colin Bell, the noted and successful radio host who is also a large man of ample proportions and with a face as red as his hair. His visage became progressively more scarlet as he struggled to read his autocue and to stay approximately perpendicular. The strain on Bell was considerable – so considerable that after a particularly fraught episode during a Conservative Party Political Conference, he appeared to fall asleep during an interview. Which was fair enough as the programme was judged by insomniacs everywhere to guarantee a good night's sleep faster and better than sheep or sleeping pills. Mr Bell left the programme soon afterwards, stuck to radio and has resolutely stayed awake and away from TV ever since.

Worst Exit from a Political Gathering

Colin Mackay, the political pundit, late of STV and now also working for BBC Radio, has always been a popular speaker and is much in demand by businessmen and fledgling politicians for his wit and wisdom on the business of being on the box. He has been known to enjoy a wee refreshment to keep his throat oiled while doing his turn, which may or may not explain why, after wooing a gathering of Conservatives, he exited smartly – straight into a cupboard, where he enjoyed a colourful (expletive deleted) close encounter with a mop and two pails. It was the hit of the evening. At least Mackay managed to leave more or less on time.

Not so Bob Cuddihy, now a media consultant but then working for STV. Bob so enjoyed the Scottish Tory Party Conference in 1986, that he failed to leave until two days after the jamboree was over.

Worst Political Party

In 1979 Jim Sillars, along with considerable numbers of the chattering classes, formed the Scottish Labour Party which promised to produce both Socialism and Devolution for Scotland. It did neither. But the Scottish Prohibition Party, born in 1901 in Dundee, was worse. It promised sobriety and separation from the demon drink. For a time it even seemed it might succeed, especially when its leading light, Edwin Scrymgeor, ejected that dedicated non-teetotaller, Winston Churchill, from his Dundee Constituency in 1922.

Worst Scottish Labour Leader – at least for Labour Votes

James Ramsay MacDonald, the illegitimate son of a ploughman and Mary Ramsay, was born in 1866 in his grannie's tiny cottage in Lossiemouth. He did not repeat his mother's mistake and married well – to Margaret Ethel Gladstone, great-niece of Lord Kelvin and daughter to the co-founder of the YMCA, Dr John Gladstone. Although she died within fifteen years of their marriage, she not only gave him six children but gave him the financial

independence which allowed him to pursue his political career. He served as Prime Minister in the first minority Labour Government in 1923 and in the second from 1929–31 but when he formed a National Government in coalition with the hated Conservatives, he was reviled and rejected by his Party.

Worst Municipal Travellers

If Motherwell Council didn't exist (which it still does, just until the unitary authorities kick in in 1996) they would have to invent it. Or Monklands. Anyway Motherwell's antics have added to the gaiety of the nation for many years although their travails on behalf of their constituents have not always been terribly well received by those who pay the municipal taxes.

Or maybe that should be, 'their travels'.

For no Council has ever surpassed Motherwell in the number and diversity of the trips it must make in foreign climes.

Always, of course, in the best interests of its electors.

No-one has been more assiduous in his duty than Vincent Mathieson, dubbed no doubt grossly unfairly by the tabloids as the 'Councillor with a suitcase', after he managed three foreign trips – to Bavaria, Norway and France – in the first half of 1991 alone.

Meanwhile colleagues managed to spend some £76,000 as they tirelessly toiled in Australia, America and Japan.

Or as Rikki Fulton said at the time, 'They've been round the world in 80 ways.'

Unfortunately not everyone saw the joke.

But all those who had ever questioned the Council's efforts were effectively silenced when, in 1994, they saw the fruits of all their Labour, when Hamilton, the neighbouring Council produced a glossy brochure, hymning the many tourists treats of their town.

But of course they realised PDQ that most foreign tourists would not have heard of Hamilton far less recognise pictures of it.

Then inspiration hit – because they knew that there could be few people living anywhere in the world who, thanks to Councillor Mathieson and his suitcase, had not heard of Motherwell . . . so they bunged photos of it on the front cover instead.

Worst Rotten Burgh

Monklands. No explanation necessary. Indeed to date, no explanation.

Worst Referendum

It wasn't so much the result of the 1979 *Referendum on the Constitution* which makes it the worst, but that 'forty per-cent' rule, thought up by George Cunningham, the Scottish MP with the English seat. If first-past-the-post was good enough to get him – and every other MP – elected, it didn't seem right or fair that the majority of Scots who voted for Devolution should then be denied it.

Worst Political Question

Tam Dalyell's West Lothian one. If only because it has been asked so often.

Worst Political Answer

Roy Hattersley, the journalist who occasionally moonlighted as an MP and was for a time Deputy Leader of the Labour Party, was interviewed by *Citizens*, the magazine of 'Charter 88', the chattering classes' favourite cause which campaigns for a written constitution for GB Ltd. When asked about Devolution Mr Hattersley sagely replied,

> 'I propose that we create Regions which have real powers. There could be, for example, a different educational system granted to Scotland. But these powers will be granted to them by Parliament. It can't possibly be a secession with Scotland simply announcing that they're taking all these powers. Westminster has to give these powers to Scotland . . .'

Absolutely.

I wonder if they'll ever give us a separate Legal system too? Or even permission for our very own Church of Scotland?

Worst Tokenism

Tony Benn was chairing a Labour meeting and declared that, in the interests of balance, he would ask questions alternately from men and women. This worked well until all the women had asked a question. Benn sipped his tea and then asked, 'Is there anyone here from Scotland?'

Worst Letter from an Unhappy Constituent

MPs have a heavy postbag to which they conscientiously reply. No-one is more assiduous in this task than Lord James Douglas-Hamilton, the terribly nice Tory MP for Edinburgh West. When he was the Minister at the Scottish Office in charge of Lauren Ordure he was no less punctilious. So when a missive arrived in his office complaining at some length about vandalism and other general anti-social behaviour, the Lord replied immediately. The fact that the letter was signed, 'Mummy,' had absolutely nothing to do with it.

Worst Act

The worst Act would appear to be the Forbes Mackenzie Act of 1853 which closed all pubs and licensed premises on Sundays. Except for so-called Bona Fide travellers which led to considerable traffic jams on the highways and byways (not to mention accidents) as drouthy drinkers Bona Fided their way up and down the country in considerable numbers. It also led directly to Scotland's morose and uncivilised public houses which were little more than drinking dens and remained so until 1976 when the licensing laws were relaxed and the Scots (or at least some of them) learned to drink for pleasure rather than to get banjaxed.

Worst Political Traitor

Of course it always depends on how you look upon these things. I mean I shouldn't think that the Labour Party was terribly pleased when Robert McLennan MP left them for the SDLP any more than they would have sent congratulatory telegrams to Jim Sillars and Dick Douglas when they packed their political bags and decamped to the SNP. There again, their new parties saw the men as true heroes and men of principle.

Even those who colluded in the death of Scotland's sovereignty in 1707 can be viewed, at least by some, in two ways.

So they are either that parcel of rogues or, alternately persons of foresight who merely anticipated the inevitable and if they managed to make themselves a few pennies along the way good luck to them.

It can be argued too that Robert The Bruce was an *arriviste*, always with an eye on the main chance who sold our very own Celtic Che Guevara, William Wallace, down the river.

And what about The Campbells whose clan and chief have not always seemed to have had Scotland's best interests at heart? After all in 1995, the current Duke was busy maintaining on TV that the defeat at Culloden was really an awfully good thing for the country. He may very well have been right because arguably Charles Edward Stuart was our worst traitor. Because not only did he lay waste the country for his ambitions but he gifted us the deadly love for the romantic loser from which we are still recovering.

Worst Parliament

It is a very long time since Scotland had a Parliament to call its own – although we do have two Parliament buildings, one in the Royal Mile and the other in the old Royal High School. In the latter of course no Parliament has ever sat, although the Scottish Grand Committee has done the occasional awayday on its blue seats. As for the former, which has been happily annexed by the Judiciary, it last sat in 1707 when it voted for its own death.

Probably the worst Parliament – at least as far as the politicians were concerned, was held in neither of these buildings but in the Canongate in 1571, where they were summoned by the Regent.

It was known as the 'creeping parliament,' not on account of any sycophancy to the Regency but because it was constantly under fire from the Catholics up the road in Edinburgh Castle and had to conduct its business on its knees.

Religious and Medical

Religion

Religion in Scotland is not unlike politics. It isn't only that in lieu of a Parliament we have the fathers and brethren (and these days, the mothers and sistren) of the annual General Assembly in New College. It is equally true that in the pursuit of religion, Scotland has probably known and has caused more schisms, sects and disruptions than even the political parties themselves.

The Presbyterians are particularly keen on Disruptions. The greatest, if not worst was in 1843 when one hundred and ninety Ministers walked out of the General Assembly and set up their own alternative which became the Free Church of Scotland. The principle involved was that of patronage. In other words the breakaway brethren were not willing to allow the Laird to continue to impose his candidate on a Parish, without reference to the congregation or its wishes. Under its first Moderator, Thomas Chalmers, the rebels attracted a third of the country's clergy away from the Church of Scotland which was considerably weakened morally, financially and spiritually.

The Free Church itself split into the Free Presbyterian Church and Free Church (the Wee Frees) in 1900. Quite what the difference between them is I do not know. Both go in for very long sermons, unaccompanied psalms and all, as the majority of their communicants are in the Isles and the Highlands, frequently in Gaelic.

I am sure that God is glad they are on his side rather than against him and in His name do deeply spiritual things like making sure the children's swings in Stornoway are safely locked up on the Sabbath lest the sound of a child's laugh disturb Him.

Worst Sect

Although not quite in the same league as the Japanese 'Ohm'

who have been accused of the gassings in the Japanese Underground, the Buchanites in the eighteenth century are in a class of their own in Scotland. (America outreligions us all. But then an awful lot of Scots did go to America . . .)

(Anyway), Mrs Buchan, a dyer's wife from Glasgow, caused amazing numbers of her followers to believe that they could get into Heaven without having to go through with all the vexatious business of bothering to die first. All they had to do was to shave their heads, keeping only a single long tuft on top of their heads. Then they would climb up to the summit of specially built platforms and wait for the angels to grab said tufts and haul them through the pearly gates. This did not happen. In fact the platform collapsed and so did the sect; a few followers remained loyal but, as Mrs Buchan also forbade sex, it did not survive.

Worst Sin

Scotland has always been very strong on sin. In fact there is nothing our clergy enjoy more than winkling out a good sin. Or concubine. Divinity students at St Andrews in 1440 were told by their Archbishop that keeping one of these obliging ladies was just possibly not quite what their vows of celibacy included.

It was at the Reformation that sin in Scotland really got going. Any sin, especially when it was one no-one, not even James Knox – who was agin' most things including anything which might be remotely pleasurable (unless it was himself marrying comely and obedient teenagers) – might have thought of. So I am sure the great man would have fully supported the Glasgow United Free Church Presbytery's condemnation in 1907 of those dens of all the iniquities – ice cream parlours. Naturally this had nothing at all to do with the fact that so many of them were owned and operated by the Papish Italians. Of course not.

Worst Sin by a Minister

It is not recorded whether the Reverend John McQueen from Edinburgh stole his parishioner, Mrs Euphememe Scott's pet-ticoats and other unmentionable underwear for his own or for his wife's use. It could have been the latter. After all when the Very Rev. McQueen was preaching the word around 1690, the stipend was on average less than £20 Scots.

McQueen's sin, however, was not quite as serious as that

of Spott's parish minister, the Rev. John Kettle who choked his wife to death and attempted to pass it off as her suicide.

But neither cleric can match the iniquities of those who connived in the Clearances, and who in the name of his Lord in heaven and his Master on earth, the Duke of Sutherland, drove the people from their lands.

NOT The Worst Sin

In 1995 the Primus of the Episcopal Church in Scotland, the Bishop of Edinburgh, the Most Rev. Richard F. Holloway caused a stushie when he suggested that the Seventh Commandment should be overhauled, if not completely overturned, as adultery was unavoidable. This was, he claimed, not because men were necessarily bad but because their genes programmed them to be unfaithful and the boys just couldn't help it.

No wonder Jenny Geddes chucked her stool when they tried to join us good Calvinists to that shower. Or not – see Worst Myth.

Worst Sermon

In May 1988, Mrs Thatcher (then Prime Minister) let it be known that she would like to address the General Assembly of the Church of Scotland. Being polite persons, they agreed – although it was a damn close run thing. When that year's Moderator, the Very Rev. James Whyte, Professor Emeritus of Practical Theology and Christian Ethics at St Andrews University, asked the gathering if it was their will that the

ST. MARGARET . . .

Prime Minister should address them, there were plenty who indicated thanks, but no thanks and gave her the Presbyterian clerical bird. However, Margaret Hilda was not to be denied and proceeded to tell the fathers and brethren of the errors of their theological ways. It was a most unfortunate cocktail of fundamentalist Conservatism mixed with the Sunday School Methodism of her youth. Even her supporters agreed that it was totally jejune, inept and inappropriate. It also went on and on . . . and on . . . for far too long, a parable, maybe, of the lady's career?

The homily became known as the Sermon On The Mound.

Worst Elder

The Church of Scotland used to be frightfully pleased that they could claim Dr Hastings Banda as one of their own brethren. Dr Banda was elected an elder while studying Medicine in Edinburgh before his country, Malawi, (formerly Nyasaland) gained independence from Britain. But as his excesses in Malawi as an absolute dictator became known, the Church became rather less keen on the connection. It became clear that many of those Banda was terrorising and even causing to disappear were themselves ministers.

Our elders at home have not been averse to the occasional bit of terrorising themselves. In the 1580s elders in the Perth parishes were excused the morning service so that they could go instead to the town's inns and taverns, not to drink, but to take down the names of all those who were, and to fine them twenty shillings. Not a small sum.

Worst Missionary

The first missionary was the worst. No doubt it was all done with the best of intentions towards the heathen and all that. But really it would have been better if they had stayed at home and done their missionary work amongst their own instead of forcing alien customs, not to mention corsets, on people who had no need of either.

Mind you Johnson, Masters and other sexologists must be deeply grateful to them for their position.

Worst Church Officer

In 1660 William Watson, a Glasgow Beadle was found to be so incapacitated with the drink as to be incapable of carrying out his duties during the service. He was punished by being made to stand and apologise to God and the congregation in his underwear, a great humiliation for such a personage.

Worst Christening

Naming the child is always an occasion fraught with diffi-culty. Babies dislike having cold water chucked over them by strange men in even stranger places.

Then there is the matter of the name itself. Pity poor Habbakuk Bisset WS and esteemed author of a book on Scots Law. He got the name courtesy of Mary Queen of Scots. His father was her caterer, and he begged the Queen to choose his new infant son's name. Mary was in a rush and impatient but she opened her Bible and selected the first name she came across, Habbakuk.

In more recent times there was the child who very nearly got called Pandora. It was not exactly a usual name in Maryhill but the Priest was used to Kylies and Chelseas and Jades, so when he asked what he should name the child and its father said Pandora he was not all that surprised. Until just as the blessing and holy water were about to fall the father tugged at his sleeve,

'Naw, naw,' he whispered, 'I said the wean's name was pinned oan' her shawl . . .'

Worst Sunday School Teacher

In 1995 Lesley Craise, a single forty-year-old lesbian and Sunday School teacher shocked Biggar Kirk to its core when she told her class that God should not necessarily be thought of as a man with a long white beard. Although Ms Craise did not go on to say that He . . . sorry, *She* was a woman in dungarees and Doc Marten's, the Session voted fourteen to thirteen that she should be asked to quit.

Worst Church Feud

Islay, as well as making very good whisky, has some very fine churches. Also it has a proper Calvinist fear of the Devil and a strong sense of sin. Their Church at Bowmore is round so that there is never a corner in which either may secrete themselves.

Portnahaven and Port Wemyss, those Siamese twins of

villages, are pushed together on the Island's western tip. They share at the top of their joint brae a joint Church, where, on a Sunday they worship a joint God and jointly sing the same hymns and listen to the same sermon. But they enter through different doors which sit side-by-side, the left for the Portnahaven, the right for Port Wemyss. Hell, one understands is inevitable for anyone foolish enough to go in the wrong door.

Who can understand the current stushie between the Free Presbyterians and the Associated Presbyterians who associate with very few and certainly not the FPs? It all began back in 1989. The major churches may go in for ecumenism but Wee Frees are made of altogether sterner stuff and of course adhering as they do to the true faith, will have none of it. Lord Mackay, the Lord Chancellor, found this out when he, although a communicant and elder in the FPs, whose closest religious chums possibly share views of the Iranian Ayatollahs, attended a Roman Catholic Requiem Mass at Westminster Cathedral. This heinous crime of listening to the words of the Harlot Church of Rome (copyright Free Presbyterians) inevitably led to his Lordship being censured and disciplined. It also led to the schism when liberals within the FPs who felt aggrieved at Mackay's treatment broke away and set up the Associated Presbyterians. Ever since, they have been happily locked in a battle with their former brethren over the ownership of Church property, including manses.

God knows why. And Mammon.

Worst Burial

Three East Lothian villages wished to claim the corpse of St Baldred, not only for reasons of piety, but because in medieval times, the shrine business was big business. It attracted lots of pilgrims and their loot. So, long and loud the battle raged until, 'lo!' a miracle and the Saint did the business. He obligingly turned his remains into three complete bodies so that Auldhame, Tyninghame and Preston could ALL have their very own cadaver. And a nice variation on the 'Feeding of the Five Thousand'.

Worst Gravestone

It's always a tricky business trying to strike the best note on the gravestone. Sometimes it's missed altogether:

Erected to the memory of
John MacFarlane
Drowned in the Water of Leith
By a few Affectionate Friends.

and

'Here Lies Andra McPherson,
Who was a peculiar person
He was six feet two
Without his shoe
And he was slew
At Waterloo.'

Worst Use of a Church

It is an unfortunate fact that there are now simply too many
church buildings. Populations have moved away from the
city centres – but then populations have moved wholesale
away from Church; only around one in ten people now go
at all, and even then only fitfully. Churches are large and
built for large congregations. To compound the problem,
many of them were built by famous architects and cannot
simply be demolished; but some are. The forty-two strong
congregation of Milton Free Church in Glasgow agreed in
1995 that they could no longer afford to keep their building
in any sort of repair. So they knocked it down. I don't know
what God thought but Glasgow District Council's Planning
Committee took a very dim view. They have taken the
Congregation collectively to Court. Quite what the outcome
will be remains to be seen. I mean, it is not like Ally McCoist's
wall (see Sport, p.00). They can hardly demand that they
restore the site to its original condition. Building back an
enormous Church complete with spire is not awfully easy.

But without demolition many of the rest are left to
fall down by themselves; giant jagged, broken tombstones
commemorating the very death of religion itself. Yet some
do live on in new disguises. Sad is the Church which gets its
P45 and becomes a pine furniture emporium, as in Church
Street in Glasgow's West End, or carpet saleroom or electricity
substation. Those that get turned into houses or even hotels,
like the one at Ballater, are surely more fortunate. And the odd

one does get passed on to another religion. It must think it has died and gone to Nirvana.

The worst fate of any church is the fate of the magnificent but redundant Catholic and Apostolic Church in Edinburgh's East London Street, at Canonmills, whose murals by the renowned Phoebe Traquair flake daily from its soaring walls. During the Edinburgh Festival it becomes, briefly, a performance space and café (even if calling it *Café Graffiti* is hardly a fitting tribute to Ms Traquair's talent). Which is bad enough but, in December where once they sang the hymns and preached the word, they now sell Christmas trees.

Worst Congregation

Around 1700 A.D. the congregation at Tulloch, near Ballater, grew weary one morning of waiting for their minister to attend to their spiritual health. It was winter and very cold. Fortunately it was also a Communion Service. So they drank the wine and began stamping and clapping their feet in the Kirk to get back the circulation. This had two results: the Reel of Tulloch was born, and when the Minister finally joined his boozy flock, he expelled the lot and refused them Communion. Furthermore, as we all know, God works in mysterious ways so that by the end of the winter, all those who had participated turned up their toes and reeled into the Churchyard in their coffins. That, as they say, will learn them. Personally, I think someone should have checked out the wine.

Worst Religious Misconception

The Rev. Robert Kirk, a fortunate name for a minister, had an unfortunate end. He had charge of the Balquhidder and Aberfoyle Parishes and claimed that he had died (temporarily) and been transported not to St Peter, but to Titania. In other words he went quite literally to the fairies who, he claimed, had kidnapped him. Or so he said. He even wrote a book about it.

John Damian, a friar in the early sixteenth century, also attempted a spot of flying. Although he got somewhat nearer to Icarus than God when the feathers in which he encased himself didn't turn him into a birdman. His attempt at Stirling Castle was watched by an interested James IV who seems to have accepted Damian's explanation that he had used the wrong sort of feathers. The King still went on to make him Abbot of Tongland.

Worst Religious Myth

Jenny Geddes did NOT throw her stool at the Bishop of Edinburgh for daring to allow mass to be said in St Giles. If it was done at all the furniture was flung by a Mrs Mean, wife of an Edinburgh Merchant.

Nor, according to every single poor reporter who was sent down every single May to check out Mrs Dora Noyce's famed (now closed) brothel in Edinburgh's Danube Street, did trade noticeably increase during the General Assembly of the Church of Scotland.

Worst Liberty with a Ministerial Name

One of the great preachers agin' the demon drink was the Rev. John Witherspoon who died in 1794 in Princeton, America, rather than in his native Paisley. Despite emigration and even his stint as a Congressman he has always been acclaimed by the town as one of its more renowned buddies. Two hundred years after his demise, the Leisure Services Committee in Paisley decided it was time they gave their famous temperance son his due and a lasting memorial. And so it came to pass that they named the PUB inside the local Arts centre, the *Rev Spoons*. The name was dropped after a public outcry from unreconstructed Rechabites.

Worst Minister

Ayrshire Presbytery's favourite son, the late Rev. James Currie, was a good man. Or at least as good a man as anyone who supports both Robert Burns and Glasgow Rangers can be. But at least he had the full support of his congregation. By contrast, there is the sad case of the minister called to take over the parish in Skye. There had always been almost a dead heat for the vacant position between two rival candidates. When the victor preached his first sermon, approximately half the congregation drowned out his words by stamping their feet and reading aloud from their Bibles. They didn't evict him.

Which is more than can be said of those ministers who assisted in the Highland Clearances, particularly the Rev. Smith who did the Duke of Sutherland's dirty work for him and drove the people from the land with his Bible in his hand and his sinecure secured by the Duke.

Worst-named Cleric

It is alleged that there was once a divinity student at New College, Edinburgh who had been cruelly (although who, apart from his loved ones, can tell) christened Biggar Balls.

But help was at hand when he flew the Presbyterian coop and ended up in with the Episcopalians where after due time and preferment he became Canon Balls.

Matters Medical

Scotland has always been proud – and rightly so – of its contribution to modern medicine. It has more ancient traditions too. In medieval times our monasteries not only grew the medicinal herbs and healing plants which provided their lotions and cures but also developed the first National Health Service, treating all who sought help from their dispensaries. By 1670 the Physic Garden in Edinburgh was growing over two hundred species of native plants which produced remedies for everything from the diarrhoea to depression. They treated animals as well as humans because, monks apart, doctors usually doubled as vets. And barbers too. Not to mention distillers. In 1500 the Barbers and Surgeons of Edinburgh were given the right to make and sell aqua vitae. Which confirms what generations of Scotsmen have maintained – that strong drink is really only taken for medicinal purposes.

Women were involved in the business of doctoring and healing as well. But unfortunately, they were quite frequently called witches and burned alive for their pains. North Berwick's witch trials in the sixteenth century could have taught them a thing, not to say a spell, or two, at Salem. One Janet Horne from Dornoch was the last Scottish witch to be put to the stake in 1727. In 1843 – or nine scant years before Joseph Lister qualified as a doctor – there was a well-documented witch trial in Dingwall. Of course when women attempted to enter the profession officially, in the later nineteenth century, there were still many male doctors who thought the witch trials had not been such a bad idea at all.

Worst Cure for Baldness

The continuing male preoccupation with the hair, or rather its absence, is not some modern fad. Since the first herbalists began creating their potions, the hunt has been on for the final, definitive answer on how to stop the stuff receding and finally galloping off the scalp altogether. It was, and indeed still is, the alchemists' hairy grail. Everything from urine to Bovril has, within the last twenty years, been solemnly and sometimes expensively recommended. Just as solemnly, amazing numbers of credulous men have tested these remedies. But nothing is quite as disgusting as the seventeenth-century Scots remedy which involved pulverising baby frogs in a pestle and then massaging it onto the head. Learned debates were held on whether the frogs should first be barbecued for the best effect.

Worst Cure for Anything

There are times when the treatment seemed rather worse than the affliction. However, the Archbishop of St Andrews in 1550 swore that he was cured of a bloody and deadly flux by being hung from his heels for a week and being fed the lightly boiled flesh of new-born puppies.

Worst Doctor

Sir Walter Scott's blacksmith whom the author encountered in England practising as a much respected medical man, assured Scott that he was doing fine. But then, as the

blacksmith said, If he killed his patients, they were English so where was the harm in it?

Worst Trick

It is said that the original for *Sherlock Holmes* was Dr Joseph Bell, Professor of Medicine at Edinburgh University. One of his favourite little jokes with his students was to demonstrate the properties of urine by dipping his finger in a bottle of it. He would then suck his finger and invite his students to do the same and then comment on their observations. The students invariably spoke about the qualities they had detected in the liquid – its taste, sweetness, bitterness or whatever. Bell would then point out that actually the finger stuck in the bottle was not the finger he had sucked.

Worst Medicine

It was thought that, until well into the nineteenth century, powdered Egyptian mummy mixed with milk would allegedly cure everything from the pox to the plague. It didn't. But, no doubt, the mere thought of having to swallow it brought about some miraculous cures.

And then there was arsenic. If it wasn't quite a medicine it was certainly widely available to whiten complexions, not to mention to bump off inconvenient lovers, as was alleged in the famous not-proven case of Madeleine Smith in 1857.

Worst Dentist

In 1968, one Alistair Inverarity, known as 'Big Nalla' joined, although qualified as a dentist, the RAF. The RAF, however, were to regret his change of career when it was alleged Big Nalla was instrumental in letting loose a Sidewinder missile over West Germany and shooting down a Tornado jet. One of our Tornado jets. Which was bad enough but as it hurtled down out of the sky Inverarity was reputed to have shouted, 'Tally Ho'. He returned to extracting molars not terribly long afterwards.

But at the tooth pulling itself, the worst was surely James IV who was so desperate for patients on whom he could practise, that he paid any of his subjects willing to have him extract their gnashers for the princely sum of fourteen shillings.

Worst Medical Habit

In the days before refrigeration, keeping bodies fresh for medical students and anatomists was a problem until some-one had the bright idea of keeping the cadavers fresh in barrels of cheap whisky. The distillers were delighted at this lucrative sideline. I don't know if they sold the spirit when the bodies were finished with it.

Worst-named Royal Doctor

Robert the Bruce employed as his chief physician a Mr Macbeth.

Worst Choice of Music

The latest thing in the operating theatre is music – which is supposed to calm the nerves as the patients go under the anaesthetic.

The choice of tunes is, however, crucial.

As Glasgow lawyer Graham Davidson found when, in the autumn of 1995, he subjected himself to the knife and a vasectomy.

As he was wheeled in the Pointer Sisters were singing *Slowhand*, which includes the refrain, 'I need a lover with a slow hand, I need a lover with an easy touch . . .' which was smartly followed by Boy George and, 'Do you really want to hurt me.'

The Surgeon Fletcher Deane is known for his sense of humour.

And Mr Davidson's operation was successful.

Trade and Industry

This is one area in which the Scots have actually done rather well is commerce. At least, we did well when we got past the Darien Venture whereby investors were convinced that sinking their bawbees into a plan which included exporting thick woollen stockings, heavy plaids and wigs deep into the hot and humid interior of Central America was a surefire winner. But in subsequent years, thanks to the happy accident of our geology, the country found itself replete with the raw materials necessary for the first Industrial Revolution. Our great coal and iron ores fuelled the furnaces of commerce and the age of steam. We were a people replete with the men who could invent as well as build this revolution. Our engineers crafted railways, waterways and ships for Britain, its Empire and the world beyond. It was glory, glory all the way, if only for those at the top of this industrial heap. They did have the odd failure. Serious ones like the collapse of the Tay Railway Bridge – and less tragic ones – including the demise of Henry Bell's pier at Helensburgh. Bell may have been able to construct Scotland's first steamship the *Comet*, but his contraption on the coast washed away on the first tide.

Yet, for all that, it was the platinum age for Scotland's industry. Even if those down at the bottom, living in the gimcrack tenements thrown up in Glasgow, Dundee and the other satanic Macmills might not have seen it quite like that. One hundred and twenty-four men perished in 1883 in Scotland's worst shipbuilding accident when Alexander Stephenson and Son's yard prematurely launched the *Daphne* which immediately sank with the workers still aboard. Their relatives, who received scant compensation, were not exactly thrilled when the ship was refloated and resurrected (and sold) as the *Rose*.

However, it was the mines which cost most lives. Accidents were only too frequent and became so common that they were barely reported, although the 1877 Blantyre Pit Explosion in which more than two hundred miners died,

took and retains the grisly title of the country's worst mining disaster. It did excite comment and relief funds for its widows and orphans were forthcoming.

Meanwhile as the Scots approached this century they invented almost everything necessary to take us into the modern age from the telephone to television. There are those who think those two machines might very well have been better left uninvented. There are even some who say that John Logie Baird didn't invent the TV at all, or at least not one which actually worked in a commercial sense.

There is also oil. It currently pumps £2 million-worth each and every hour into the British Treasury. It leads some to say that this has not been entirely to Scotland's benefit – as we are the only country not to have been considerably enriched by the discovery of the black gold within its territorial jurisdiction. But, as in all things, it depends how you look upon it and Kuwait may well disagree with this assessment.

In the name of industry and development we have both imported and exported things animal, vegetable and mineral which have not necessarily been to the general betterment of mankind.

Worst Navvies

Our industrial infrastructure may have been designed by highly educated and clever men but it was all physically – and at great cost – built by armies of itinerant navvies, many from Ireland, but also from among Scotland's own labouring classes. It was a hard and hazardous life. Many died. But two illustrious Ulstermen survived to find more rewarding work. Messrs Burke and Hare were navvies who dug the Union Canal before they got down to the more profitable business of digging up bodies for the Edinburgh anatomists and necromancers.

Worst Import

Although there may be others on two legs which have destroyed and laid waste vast tracks of the Highlands and Islands few have done more damage than the Black-Faced Ewe whose importation led directly to the clearances. Which leads us to . . .

Worst Exports

The 'Ku Klux Klan' which was formed from some of the Scottish Diaspora driven from the land by the sheep to America.

If the Klan did not come directly from Scotland, Jardine Matheson, the great Hong Kong trading conglomerate most definitely did. The company, which made more junkies and more money from opium, than the entire Mafia, was founded by James Matheson from Lairg and his partner William Jardine of Lochmaben.

And despite Al Capone and his lieutenants' murderous activities, the official Mafia never caused a war either; unlike the Jardine Matheson mandarins. Although the Opium Wars of the 1840s did give Britain Hong Kong its temporary – soon to be terminated – lease of the Colony.

Worst Industrialist

Not content with ruining the health of thousands of Glaswegians with the noxious fumes of his chemical works, Lord Overtoun, the nineteenth-century Bible-thumping magnate felt called, not only to export his allegedly Christian evangelical fervour but his industrial fever to (the then) Nyasaland, thus ruining both its indigenous customs and commerce. He was a dictator who wrapped his absolute power in piety which made it even less acceptable. His Lordship was a touch too extreme, even for the strong nerves of his contemporary industrial privateers. When he died his obituary by Alexander Petrie in the *Clincher* carried the headline, 'Consternation in Heaven – Lord Overtoun failed to arrive'.

Worst Industrial Disaster

Just as the Darien Venture was disastrous for the nation
in 1700, the decision by Government to develop a motor
industry at Linwood and at Bathgate were equally calamitous
for the country in the postwar years. It might just have worked
if they had also built up a components industry at the same
time or within a reasonable distance of either plant. This
small, if essential, matter, was wholly overlooked by the
politicians of all parties who didn't seem to grasp that
having to transport practically everything, which makes up
the modern motor car from far-off factories in the South,
could possibly scupper the whole grandiose plan. It did.

The schemes for the Highlands were hardly more successful. Lord Leverhulme the soap king from Bolton who
bought Lewis and Harris in 1918 and spent £875,000 in his
attempt to turn the islands into industrial paradises was not
the only one who failed. His abandonment of Lewis five years
later led directly to the emigration of more than one thousand
of that island's brightest and best. Harris fared little better
although it enjoyed a brief boom when the tiny settlement
of Obbe became the busy harbour of Leverhulme. But when
the magnate died in 1925, so did all his plans and schemes,
and the islanders' artificial prosperity along with them.

Forty years later, public money did little better in trying
to bring new industry northwards. From the pulp mill at
Corpach to the aluminium smelter, they failed, and led
inevitably to a new round of clearances.

There was a whole village constructed for the workers at
the Oil Rig Yard at Portavadie in Argyll . . . The houses got
built. Lots of them. But the rigs and the jobs did not appear
because by the time they had put the last coat of paint on
the would-be homes, there was a glut of yards and a dearth
of platforms to be built. There were attempts to sell the whole
expensive fiasco as a 'Highland Hi-di-Hi' holiday camp, but,
to date, there have been no takers. The place rots on as a
monument to misplaced planning and general government
incompetence. It cost the taxpayer some £76 million.

Recently, the Scottish Office, having learned nothing,
has been busy handing out £38 million more in grants
to 'Health Care International' to build and equip a private
hospital at Clydebank. HCI's supporters persuaded Ian Lang
(Scottish Secretary at that time) that health-care was a

growth business and that patients would be flown in for their hernias and heart by-passes from all over the world. This illusion collapsed within a couple of months and the hospital was sold on to another group – at a knock-down price.

Worst Motor Car

The 'Hillman Imp' that pale if slightly more sophisticated imitation of the sexier 'Austin Mini' first driven off the production line at Linwood by Prince Philip in 1961, was born to fail.

The parent company realised fairly early on that it was unlikely to have a long garage life. Having it made in faraway Scotland with the help of government grants and much brouhaha about the regeneration of the Scottish Motor Industry didn't help its survival. Nor did it keep the Labour Party, whose brainchild it was, in power.

Worst-appreciated Invention

In Milngavie, if you search hard enough, can still be found the remains of the 'Bennie Railplane'. This wonder was the invention of George Bennie who in 1930 erected a quarter mile of overhead track on which his train was predicted to be capable of reaching two hundred miles an hour.

Although it attracted worldwide attention and acclaim when it was inaugurated, it did not manage to rake in sufficient financial support from investors. Bennie quickly became bankrupt.

It was a stunning technological achievement and inno-vation which was, of course, chucked away because of lack of foresight and imagination – an auld sang and one which has been sung too often by Scotland's inventors.

Worst Luck with an Invention

Even more unfortunate than Bennie was the Aberdonian Sandy Fowler. In 1945 while working in the tea industry in Ceylon, he invented the teabag. His wife ran up the first batch on her Singer sewing machine (now there was an invention which was properly exploited) but no-one seemed particularly interested. As Mr Fowler himself wasn't entirely convinced about the merits of his bright idea, he sold the rights for £1500.

Fifty years on and trillions of teabags later, his invention

IGNORE WEE HAMISH –
IT'S ONLY THE POSTMAN!

having made fortunes for the tea companies, it was decided to hold a giant party in Sri Lanka to laud and praise Sandy's brainwave.

Mr Fowler, by now 81, was invited to attend. As he was then living on £35 a week he couldn't afford the fare.

Worst Invention

In July 1934 one Gerhardt Zucher prepared to demonstrate the three-foot-long rocket with which he proposed to deliver medicines and mail to Scotland's remoter islands. Special commemorative stamps were issued and a letter to George V was composed and was got ready to be blasted, along with 30,000 others, between Scarp and Harris. The rocket exploded, as did the letters which landed alright – as confetti.

Worst Gold Rush

Whatever the truth about the benefits or otherwise of black gold, Scotland does have the distinction of having the worst gold rush. Not before she lost tens of thousands of people to those rather larger affairs in California in 1849 and in Australia a couple of years later. Some of those lacking the passage money and who stayed in Scotland, rushed instead, in 1868, to Ullie in Sutherland when it was revealed that there was gold in them thar Straths. In fact, all of four-hundred prospectors took their picks and pans north and hoped to make their fortunes. Only 600 ounces were ever found before the Duke of Sutherland (no, not *that* one this time) closed the workings down, not because he didn't want to share the loot with less wealthy men, but because his tenants and the locals complained that all the activity was interfering with the sheep. As we all know, nothing is allowed to interfere with them.

Worst Road

The Muirkirk to Sanquhar road may appear on some old maps but does not, in fact, exist and, although planned, it was never built.

Just as odd offshoots and flyovers to nowhere have, for some time, been a feature of the motorway system in Glasgow. As everyone who spent most of 1994 and 1995 trying to get in or out of the wretched city knows, these are now being completed with the help of EU money and grants, causing massive tailbacks and holdups on the approach roads. Whether this will eventually benefit Glasgow remains to be seen. The money might have been better spent on doing something about the A1 South which remains, in part, a three-lane death trap which kills and injures more drivers and passengers than any other road in GB.

The worst road of them all is any road at all in Edinburgh city centre. By widening the pavements and narrowing traffic lanes, they have successfully introduced almost permanent gridlock to the whole of the capital. Well done those planners!

Worst Bridge

To state the obvious, the first Railway Bridge over the Tay was not exactly an unqualified success but at least it fulfilled its function, if only for a while. Unlike the Ashtiel Bridge over the Tweed, constructed by John and Thomas Smith, the famous Borders engineers, in 1847. When the final keystone was inserted in its single arch, the whole edifice fell into the river. I do not think that it is entirely true that there are certain sections of the community in Skye who prayed that something similar might happen to the Skye Bridge.

Worst Industrial Con

Whatever the merits or demerits of nuclear power, the frequent TV adverts, not to mention those omnipresent on

the sides of buses and in the press, extolling the wonders of Torness, are a brilliant and terrifying example of the black art of propaganda. By suggesting that Torness is little more than a nice awayday for the kiddies, healthily set by the seaside and in the countryside, British Nuclear have managed to convince sizeable numbers of people that they are engaged in nothing more menacing than any other tourist attraction, something like 'Deep Sea World' maybe or perhaps a Hydroelectric Plant.

I wonder if Five-Mile Island in the States ever ran anything similar?

Worst Industrial Fault

Blaming everything which goes wrong on the English. Even if it's true.

Worst Industrial Detritus

When an industry dies it leaves its own memorials. Some are silent but bring death – like the pneumoconiosis from the mines and the cancer from white asbestos, used with such profligacy in the building industry in the past. Others are more visible in gap-sites and razed factories whose willowherb-strewn wastelands show the demise of industrial dreams.

There are the oil-shale bings, those relics of 'Paraffin' Young, fellow student of David Livingstone at Glasgow's Anderson College who found it more profitable to explore the Lothians than Africa in search of oil-rich shale. There is little that is less lovely than an oil-shale bing, which surely makes it all the more astonishing that bordering the M8, and fronting the Livingston Mitsubishi factory, there should be three approximations of these monstrous mounds which were deliberately built in the name of art.

Banking

As every schoolchild knows it was a Scotsman, William Paterson, who founded the Bank of England in 1694. The Bank itself tends to dispute this, but that's the English for you. And Banks – they seldom accept their liabilities. Whatever the truth of Paterson's claim, one year later in 1695, the Bank of Scotland was definitely created by an Englishman, John Holland and was followed fairly quickly by the Royal, the British Linen and the Union and Clydesdale Banks as well as the various Savings Banks which began in Ruthwell in Dumfriesshire in 1810 when the local minister, Rev. Henry Duncan set one up for his parishioners.

Unlike the commercial banks, they did not lend money to business or issue their own notes.

Soon the movement spread throughout the whole country and contributed hugely to the Scots' reputation as a thrifty nation with moths in its sporrans. This unfairly led to one of the worst myths and calumnies put about by our enemies. We give more to charity *per capita* and spend more on the National Lottery than the English, Welsh or Irish.

However the worst banking myth of all is that the Scottish Banks' notes are legal tender. They are not. But don't tell anybody.

Worst Banker

John Law, the son of a wealthy goldsmith, was born in 1671 in Edinburgh where he attended the High School.

He was fascinated by figures and gambling.

But also by women.

Having removed himself and his financial expertise to London he killed another man in a duel over a lady and was forced to flee to the Continent.

In Holland and Italy he devoted himself to studying everything available on the fledgling banking systems then operating – although he also found time to elope with someone else's wife.

He returned briefly to Scotland at the beginning of the

18th century and offered to reform the country's whole economy.

Thanks but no thanks he was told and he removed himself in a huff to France which did accept his ideas.

At first everything went along absolutely splendidly and both France and he profited enormously.

He was elected a member of the Academie Française and became Comptroller-General of the nation's finances in 1720.

Almost immediately the currency collapsed, the economy was in ruins, and all in all the financial chaos and misery which prevailed led almost inevitably to the French Revolution and the Terror.

After the fiasco Law fled again, this time to Italy where he died soon afterwards.

Rich.

Worst Bank Crash

Glasgow has been unluckier than most in its experience with banks. In 1857 the Western Bank with one hundred branches went down with liabilities of £9 million. In 1878, the City of Glasgow Bank managed to ruin approximately 1600 depositors when it closed its doors. It was of course Edinburgh's fault. Her hard-nosed financiers passed the rap as well as the port and refused to bail them out.

Matters Military

It has been said that countries without histories are the only happy ones. Who, having examined the long chronicles of Scotland's glorious and inglorious past could disagree? From Flodden to Culloden, through Stewarts and stewards, we have had our share of history, and then some.

Not, of course, that everyone including the natives is actually aware of it. Whole generations grew up knowing the complete genealogy and all of the lives of the Kings and Queens of England but who, beyond a romanticisation of Mary, Queen of Scots and the fictionalisation of Macbeth, were taught little of the Scottish royal houses.

We learned our history not from cold facts in school but from old songs and older sentiments which told us that Bonnie Prince Charlie and William Wallace were good while John Knox and every Campbell was bad. *Flower of Scotland* and *Flooers o' the Forest*, victory and defeat, it was frequently difficult to disentangle the two.

But for all that, Scotland is not a *conquered* nation. For good or ill we *sold* our portion and our independence. It was never permanently taken from us on any battlefield although there were times when it was temporarily lost before James VI and I won the end-game and the joint throne.

We have exported our services. Scottish mercenaries plied their trade in every country where the prices and the Princes were right. For Scots, if not Scotland, found war a profitable business. There have been few corners of the British or other Empires without its Scottish soldiers, their bagpipes and their blood, which has led to some nice meetings and greetings. There was the occasion when the Russians and the Turks were fighting over the Crimea. After much slaughter, a temporary truce was arranged for the business of burial, between the two commanding generals. They talked terms through an interpreter, both men wearing the full finery that their rank in their respective armies demanded. The Turk was particularly magnificent, swathed in silk and jewels, including a turban set with rubies and diamonds. At the end of the negotiations, he took a long, hard stare at the Russian Commander-in-Chief and said in the unmistakable tones of the Mearns,

'Hey min, you're yon loon Keith frae Peterhead, aren't ye? Don't ye ken, I'm the bell ringer's loon frae the Bullers of Buchan . . . Hey min we've baith done affey weel, hiven't we?'

And with that he waved and went on his way to continue the slaughter. In fact the Russian General was indeed the loon frae Peterhead, James Francis Edward Keith, born at Inverugie Castle and brother of the last Earl Marischal. When he was nineteen years old, Keith joined the followers of the Old Pretender and fought at Sheriffmuir. On the failure of the campaign, he fled to Spain and their army, which he soon left for the better pickings and promotions under the Russians who always had a place for a good fighting Scotsman in their ranks. But despite becoming a General he moved on, yet again, and sold his services to the Prussians where he ended up as a Field Marshal, Governor of Berlin – and dead. In 1758 he was finally killed in a battle between his latest adopted nation and the Austrians, but his expertise was not forgotten, and just over a century later, Kaiser Wilhelm I gifted a statue of Keith to his home town of Peterhead. I cannot find any statue of the Turkish General although he was said to have pleased his boss so much that he was given his own harem. So maybe he left his own flesh and blood memorials behind.

We might also bear in mind our glorious defeats. At least five Scots died at the Alamo, one of them being John McGregor who encouraged Davie Crockett and the rest by playing the bagpipes. Maybe death wasn't quite so bad after that.

Worst Date

As far as loss of life is concerned, the worst date is not 1513 or 1746 but 1861 – which was the year in which Earl Haig, Commander-in-Chief of the British Expeditionary Forces in France between 1915–1919 was born.

Worst Insult

When General James Wolfe was discussing the merits of recruiting and expanding Highland Regiments for the British Army, he was reputed to have been convinced it was a good idea, because, as he said, mindful of his public relations,

'There would be no great mischief if they fall'.

Worst Defeats

As in football so also in war. All our most glorious failures have been at the hands or rather the arms of the English. Bannockburn was one of our few home wins when Robert the Bruce, using the four-square formation of spearsmen, made best use of the ground and drove back Edward II's less mobile lines of cavalry and infantry. But in the past we have tasted more failure than success. From Dunbar in 1296 when Surrey's army routed our boys and caused Baliol to surrender his kingdom as a direct result a year later . . . through Halidon Hill in 1333 when we lost a whole back row, five belted Earls in a one'er, and on and on to Flodden in 1513.

Flodden was a battle of two halves, when the Scots (and oh, how often have we heard the phrase before) snatched defeat out of the jaws of certain victory. We surrendered our initial tactical advantage and allowed the Anglos an easy win, in the process managing to wipe out not only the King himself, James IV, and most of his household too. It did, of course, give us that rather decent pipe tune and dirge, *The Flooers o' the Forest* (never to be confused with '*Flooers of Edinburgh*' which is about what they used to call 'night soil' and which was flung from the privies into the capital's streets below) although a song was hardly adequate compensation.

Cromwell also played a blinder and smashed David Leslie's Scottish troops at a rematch, three hundred and fifty odd years after the first, at Dunbar, in 1650.

There was 1746 and Culloden: Bonnie Prince Charlie versus his relative-a-little removed, the Duke of Cumberland,

otherwise known as 'The Butcher'. It was definitely the worst battle, not for the outcome, but because it is still seen as Scotland against England when in fact it was as much a 'Scotland A' versus 'Scotland B'. Contrary to myth and misconception, there were more Scots actually fighting FOR Cumberland and the Hanoverians than against him with the Jacobites.

Worst Defeats Abroad for Scottish Regiments

A scant twelve years after Culloden, in America, the Black Watch was wiped out at the battle of Ticconderoga while attempting to storm a French Fort. The Black Watch was again badly mauled in 1883 when they allowed the British square red box to be broken by the Dervishes in the Sudan. But the least glorious failure of them all was surely the shocking defeat of the professional Gordon Highlanders by a small force of farmers-turned-soldiers in 1880 during the First Boer War. Equivalent really to Rangers going down to Berwick Rangers. Which they once did, of course.

Worst Defeat in World War II

At St Valéry-en-Caux, as part of the British Expeditionary Force, the 51st Highland Division was put up as a sitting target for the German Army and thus sacrificed to allow the 'miracle' of Dunkirk. It also resulted in the famous Reel of the 51st Division which was born when, after the defeat, the captured soldiers of the regiment were incarcerated in their prison camp at Laufen. First called the Laufen or the

St Valéry Reel, it was later decided that it was hardly good for regimental morale or memory if this military disaster was commemorated by a dance. Never let it be said that British generals don't get their priorities right.

Worst Commanders

And just as all our failures in battle are glorious, so have none of our Scottish Commanders been bad – merely unlucky. All our Captains and our Kings – not least that unluckiest family of them all, The Stuarts – have had their share of ill fortune and then some. There was James II, killed by his own cannon as it fired to lift the siege on Roxburgh in 1460 – surely an early incidence of that military miscalculation known as 'friendly fire'. James III didn't do much better when he was murdered by persons unknown after fleeing the field at Sauchieburn and the victorious army led by his son, James IV.

It had been foretold that he would be betrayed by his nearest if not dearest and to safeguard himself James Three had had his brothers locked up and thus committed his own worst mistake.

But apart from the Stuarts and Haig, the worst commander is the Earl of Mar who, in 1715, managed to turn an unassailable position into defeat at Sheriffmuir. Mar, known as 'Bobbing John' for his habit of changing sides, raised the Standard for the Old Pretender at Braemar and marched southwards to meet up with the much smaller force of pro-Hanoverians.

Sheriffmuir was like one of those matches where Scotland plays a part-time team made up from housepainters and joiners and expects to walk it – but ends up with a 0–0 draw which is bad enough in itself but stops them progressing towards some bigger tournament.

So it was at the 1715 battle. Both sides claimed victory but the reality was that the 1715 Rising was from that point on, finished.

Worst Military Myth

It is generally accepted that if General, later Marshal, Wade did nothing else, he built some jolly good roads in Scotland. In truth they were badly aligned, inadequately built and deteriorated extremely rapidly. Their chief purpose – to allow a rapid response force to get in at, to contain and to crush those rebellious Scots – also failed. Because their

main beneficiary was Bonnie Prince Charlie whose forces used them to some effect, advancing much more quickly than they would otherwise have done.

Worst Massacres

There's nothing like a good massacre to keep hostilities going, as everyone who knows about Glencoe understands. But dreadful though that may have been, the carnage in 1692 with only thirty-eight killed, was nothing as compared to many.

The English did their bit at Berwick and managed to slaughter thousands of people between 1296 and 1551 and caused thirteen changes of ownership. While Montrose's army in Argyll and Angus in 1645 could have shown today's Serbians a thing or two about rape and pillage and bloody murder. Still, if only because of the propaganda and the continuing folk memories which surround it to this day, Glencoe must stand supreme, despite it being in newspaper terms a smallish massacre with not many dead.

Worst Mutiny

The worst military crime is mutiny. It is something which is and was feared by every army in every age. But considering everything with which armies ancient and modern have put up with, quite the most surprising thing is that there have been so few.

Although equally surprising are the reasons for mutiny – like the one at Leith in 1779 when 50 newly recruited

Highlanders went berserk because they believed they were about to be forcibly co-opted into a GLASGOW regiment.

The troops were called out and 27 soldiers ended up dead.

However the worst and most serious mutiny of the lot was that of the Black Watch or as it was then known The 43rd Highland Regiment in 1743.

If going to Glasgow was thought to be bad, being sent to England was judged as being rather worse than getting the one-way ticket across the Styx.

And as their reward for successfully keeping peace in the Highlands for close on 15 years, the 43rd had been assured that they never would be marched across the Border. Or further afield either.

Until 1743.

Then it was decreed that they should march to London, to be reviewed by the King, George II and then dispatched to Flanders – although it was thought advisable not to mention the final part of the plan.

In the event not only did the King fail to review the regiment (which was taken as a gross insult) but they were treated by the English as if they were monkeys let loose from a zoo.

When they were told that they couldn't return to their glens, there began mass desertions and finally out-right revolt.

In the end over 100 men were charged with mutiny and desertion and after a show trial ordered to be shot.

Because of the practicalities of executing so many, and as more people, both in England and Scotland rallied to their cause, the sentences, with four exceptions, were commuted to transportation.

Patrick McGregor was ordered to receive 1000 lashes while Samuel and Malcolm McPherson, together with Farquar Shaw were made examples of and were shot.

But the death of the other mutineers was merely delayed. Soon they too perished in the foreign fields to which they had been sent and none ever again saw their hills of home.

Worst Uniform

From the time of the Napoleonic Wars many yeomanry regiments were raised by private individuals for the defence of the realm. They were a sort of Home Guard. It was also thought to be both fashionable and patriotic. Indeed it was not so very different from the habit of today's top businessmen to buy themselves into football clubs.

But they at least are not allowed to design the strip.

Unlike the 18th- and 19th-century Captain Mainwarings who spent at least as much time on choosing the uniforms for their troops as on drilling them.

But then it was a time when all men – or at least those who could afford it – were in their popinjay phase.

Many and wild were the variations, with shakos and brass buttons and gold braid galore.

But few of these outdid the so-called Fencibles (or home defence forces) raised in Scotland.

These, with their mongrel mixing of kilts with red coats, oversized sporrans and busbies were described by contemporary commentators as, 'Mockeries of Highland Dress'.

For all that they were still of their time and place which is more than can be said for the current Royal Company of Archers.

This bunch of geriatric gents, recruited entirely from the ranks of the would-be great if not entirely good, is allegedly the Queen's bodyguard in Scotland and turn up at Garden Parties at Holyrood and other ceremonial occasions done up to the nines in their tight trews and green jackets, not to mention the very long feather in their bonnets about which they are always forgetting and which gets regularly stuck in car doors.

But they are marginally better than that uniform worn by our alleged clan chiefs. In their kilts and eagle feathers, clutching their overlong cromachs, they resemble *en masse* the chorus of a cut-price touring company of *Brigadoon*.

Worst Military Oversight

When the Regimental Association of the Queen's Own Cameron Highlanders put up a cairn at Erracht near Achnacarry in 1993 to commemorate the anniversary of the founding of the Regiment in 1793 they forgot to get planning permission. It now seems that they may have to dismantle it stone by stone.

Worst Obituary

When Lt Col. Richard Broad died in 1993, the *Daily Telegraph* devoted considerable space to his obituary and tales of his regimental derring-do, including the story of his escape from the rout at St Valéry in 1940. The paper explained that he and his *English* troops built a raft to cross the Seine to relative safety. The obituary waxed lyrical about the ingenuity of these *English* Tommies but, praise where praise is due and all that, the *Telegraph* also recognised that, 'All the *Englishmen* were indebted to the French lady who helped them and their Regiment.' The English Regiment to which Broad belonged was The Seaforth Highlanders.

Worst Military Poem

There is something about the Scottish soldier which brings out the worst in both song and poetry. Andy Stewart, et al, are only the half of it. William Edmonstoune Aytoun, Professor of Rhetoric and *Belles-Lettres* (pseud? *moi?*) was a particularly fine exponent of the genre. His *Lays of Scottish Cavaliers and Other Poems* was modelled, it was said, on works by Sir Walter Scott. Need I say more, other than that they were much appreciated by Queen Victoria? The *Massacre of the MacPherson* never left a dry eye at Balmoral.

Worst Weapon

The worst weapon ever deployed against the Scots by the English in our long series of skirmishes was 'War Wolf', a fearsome machine which was trundled north by Edward in 1304 to end the siege of Stirling Castle. Actually the castle's commander, Sir John Oliphant, was quite willing to give in, but no, Edward wanted to test his new toy and refused the surrender so that his engineers could assess its capabilities.

Our own 'Mons Meg' some three-hundred and seventy-odd years later, exploded while being demonstrated to the Duke of York.

But the K boats, an early submarine at the beginning of this century with furnaces, steam engines and two funnels, both of which had to be lowered and sealed before the boats could be submerged, were infinitely more deadly. Not to the enemy of course. Nearly three-hundred men were lost in sixteen major accidents including the infamous Battle for the Isle of May in which a thirty-mile flotilla of boats was assembled by the British Navy for a secret exercise in the Firth of Forth.

During this fiasco several K boats collided with each other and with some of the surface vessels; one hundred and three men died during the chaos. Only one K boat ever actually engaged the enemy. That too was a disaster as its torpedo failed to explode. But they tried again, modified and redesigned the vessel as a submersible sea-plane carrier complete with a hangar (with watertight doors) plus a catapult to launch the planes at the enemy. That didn't work either.

Sport

Sport has not infrequently been described as a substitute for war. This is very true, as in war so also are, our sporting humiliations also glorious failures. We expect to lose. Sometimes it seems we prefer to lose. Indeed we take a proper pride in going down the sporting Swanny. There is one exception to all this – any loss against England, at anything, anywhere, is an occasion for wearing the willow, for national lachrymosity and self-laceration all round. Lamentations too. Strong men who will stay dry-eyed at the deaths of their mothers and the births of their babies will weep when the Auld Enemy puts the Adidas in their dreams. Editors of Scottish Sunday newspapers are also known to shed tears on these occasions, not necessarily because they are patriots to a person but on account of the sharp decline in sales of their sheets. We do not, apparently, like to read about our defeats. So obviously there can be no defeats included or discussed here at all. In this chapter there will be nothing but glorious and ever-yet more glorious failures . . .

Football

Probably it is best to get the worst out the way first, but deciding which of the England v. Scotland clashes in the beautiful game merits the title is not easy. It would take a statistician to work out whether it was worse for us to go down 2–7 in 1955 or 3–9 in 1961. Although there is no doubt that the title of worst goalie must remain with Frank Haffey, the gallant keeper at the latter tourney. He emigrated. To Australia.

However, despite Mr Haffey it was at Wembley in 1928 that the worst really happened when our Wizards actually beat the English 5–1 – definitely the worst result. It raised our expectations for generations and gave us the feeling that if we could do it once, we should be able, nae bother at all, to do it every time.

Worst Misses in the World Cup

When Scotland played Brazil in the 1974 World Cup, the score was 0–0 until suddenly, there in front of Billy Bremner, was the ball and just a tap away there too was an empty goal and glory – as well as entry into the next round. Billy missed and sent the fans homewards to think again about ever progressing further in this most prestigious of tournaments. It was agreed that never would Scotland ever miss a more important goal.

But as ever Scotland lived down to their expectations.

So twelve years later, in 1986 in Argentina Steve Nichol went one better when he missed what, at least on TV, looked like little more than a 4-inch tap into Uruguay's more or less unguarded goal mouth.

1994 was our best World Cup ever.

Because we didn't take part and our illusions and pretensions remained intact.

Especially as the Anglos didn't spoil it for us by winning.

Worst Football Stamp

The philatelic bureau of the Caribbean island of Grenada were so taken with the above-mentioned Mr Bremner's miss that they captured it for prosperity by issuing a stamp showing Billy clutching his head in despair.

Worst World Cup Song

Oh the potency of cheap music – and nothing comes cheaper or more awfully potent than that appalling ditty *Ally's Army* with which we convinced ourselves that the World Cup in 1978 in Argentina was a doddle. Unfortunately the song has proved less forgettable than our performance. In any pub in Scotland, at any time, day or night, you can find sizeable numbers of grown men – and women (ask journalist Ruth Wishart) – who still know every word and note of the thing.

They probably know the 1974 anthem too, including its immortal refrain,

'Yabba dabba doo, we support the boys in blue and it's easy, easy'.

Worst Football Song

It is only foul rumour and nasty anti-Rangers propaganda that certain supporters sing sectarian songs at their games. That ditty, *The Sash My Father Wore*, refers to the time when the singers' ancestor won a Miss World or possibly Mr Universe. They did once certainly sing,

'Have we told you, Hateley, that we love you?'

The Sash sounds better.

Worst Chant

After being beaten . . . after going down gloriously . . . 1–0 to Denmark in the Mexico World Cup in 1986, the Scottish fans regaled the opposition with the immortal words,

'You can stick your streaky bacon up your arse.'

Worst Gift for a Goalie

Andy Goram is the Scottish goalie who is occasionally not quite together enough or in the right mood to play for his country – but fortunately nearly always for Rangers. His inability to be in goal for the national side in their 1995 qualifier against Greece, earned him the headlines, 'GET A SHRINK, GORAM,' in the tabloids. So Ally McCoist, his club team-mate thoughtfully left a strait-jacket on Goram's peg in the club's dressing room is surely the worst gift given to a goalie.

Worst-named Supporters' Club

When Celtic fans in Bellshill named their Club in honour of

the assassinated American President, John F Kennedy, their Rangers counterparts changed their name to: 'The Lee Harvey Oswald Loyal'.

Worst-named Fanzine

One of the definite advances of the modern game has been the rise and rise of the fanzine, those daft wee magazines which were begun by supporters to counteract both the appalling standards of their Clubs' official publications and the parrot prose of the tabloids back pages (parrot prose, because they report exactly what they are told by the management).

The fanzines at their best are pertinent, impertinent, informed, prejudiced and frequently very funny indeed. Just like the game itself. Fanzines are also quirky, not least in their choice of titles. Partick Thistle's *Sick in the Basin* is hard to beat.

Worst-named Team

Difficult to choose really between Airdrieonians, retitled *Airdrie Onions*, courtesy of the UEFA official at the 1992 European Cup Winner's Cup Draw, or the BBC announcer's *Stenhousemanure*. Stenhousemuir incidentally is twinned with *Pett Bottom*, near Canterbury. No, I don't know why either.

Worst Slogan on a T-shirt

Seen outside Ibrox at the start of the 1995 season a man with a shirt bearing the legend, 'Gazza for Pope'.

Worst Substitution

During a Partick Thistle v. Hearts match, 'the Jags' manager Bertie Auld was incensed by what he perceived as his striker, Jim Melrose's lack of commitment. He ordered his assistant Pat Quinn to take him off. Quinn pointed out that Thistle had already used both subs ... but Auld took Melrose off anyway *pour encourager les autres*.

Worst Tactics

A manager of Clyde who shall remain nameless was very fond of a wee refreshment. Or ten. Just before an important game his players found him snoring away, fast asleep in the dressing room. The Captain then made a short and very moving speech along the lines that the Boss was a very nice guy, so let's go out there and do the business for him and give him a nice surprise when he wakes up.

They won too.

Worst Leaving Gift

When George Best finished his brief spell at Hibs, the Supporters' Club wanted to mark the occasion with an appropriate gift in recognition of his services and to encourage him in his continuing battle with the booze – so they gave him a whisky decanter and six glasses.

Scotland's Worst Defensive Wall

When Ally McCoist of Rangers moved to the salubrious, rural delights of Bridge of Weir, a conservation village a few miles West of Glasgow, to a house which suited his status and salary, only one thing was found wanting in his new home – privacy. So McCoist decided to erect a goal-post-high fence around his policies. He was refused permission by the planners and told to plant trees instead. But Ally always was a man in a hurry and trees are slower than a Celtic back four, so he went ahead and bunged up his wall anyway. Maybe he thought no-one would notice, especially when with low, or even high, cunning he built on top of the original one.

But although Bridge of Weir is sleepy as well as snobby and likes to keep itself to itself at all times, even *its* residents couldn't miss McCoist's folly. For one thing, as well as being extremely tall it was given to weeping white mortar all over the village every time it rained. In August 1995, the referees, in the guise of Council officials, blew their whistles and McCoist's defence was judged off-side and offensive. He was given twenty-eight days to remove it with no appeal to the SFA. Foul.

Worst International Strip

The Scottish international football team's managers and coaches may have made the odd mistake here and there in Argentina, Spain and at Hampden but their fashion sense is more error-prone still. It isn't just those funny peculiar long, bum-warming anoraks they favour for dugout wear, come rain, snow and the occasional, very occasional sun, it's their choice of strip for their players. Or not. In 1954 the players were sent to the World Cup without any official jerseys at all. Which on reflection was probably worse than that which the

SFA (Scottish Football Association) inflicted on the nation's eyeballs in 1984/85 – a confection and combination of blue and white which made every player look as if he had been forced to wear a low slung suspender belt around his middle. It was not a pretty sight. But worst of all is the current lycra tartanised effort worn by the WOMEN'S International side whose only possible virtue is that it hides their underarm sweat-marks. There is also the 1995 international men's side's away strip – in vibrant red and pulsating purple which cannot be tackled without shades and a stiff gin. No doubt that is the whole point.

Worst Moustache

Apart from pilots in the Second World War and Prussian Generals of the past there has only been one other group which continues to cling to moustaches – football managers and commentators – Jim White of Scottish Television is only the latest to assume that hair on the upper lip adds gravitas and authority. This assumption is not always true, not least when one is presenter of the worst football quiz – *A Game of Two Halves*. There was also Willie Pettigrew's Zapata in the 1970s which made him look like a refugee from a Spaghetti Western.

Willie Henderson's upper lip has had its moments, too. But if only because he had clung on to his through thick and thicker, including sundry wives, football clubs and countries, the worst 'tache ever cultivated belongs without doubt to Graham Souness. No wonder he ended up in Turkey where EVERYONE sports a moustache.

Worst-dressed Footballer

Something happens to footballers when they are allowed out on their own, and we are not only talking about the worst of Duncan Ferguson who probably deserves a whole chapter to himself and would too if it wasn't for m'learned chums in wigs – not least in the matter of their sartorial flair. But then in all fairness anyone forced to spend hours in those tracksuits and the technicolor lycra dreams of the sportswear manufacturers, is more or less bound to end up a Versace victim. And of no-one is this truer than the Ex-Ranger, Mark Hateley, whose addiction to expensive violent striped jackets must make his new fans rejoice that his eyesight appears to improve on the park. It was obviously the arrival of that

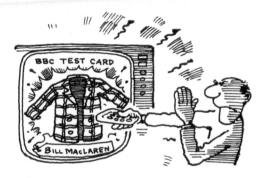

sometime bouncing bottle blond boyo from Newcastle, Mr Gascoigne, which made Mark quit for pitches new. He couldn't stand the competition for the double – worst dressed player AND worst hairstyle.

Couture crisis affects TV commentators too. Who having seen Bill McLaren's tweed jacket has not adjusted their vertical hold? People have exchanged their colour TVs for black and white sets purely to avoid Dougie Donnelly's fetching confections in pink. But Chic Young (whose relationship to fashion is not dissimilar to Scottish forwards relationship to goal-posts by going way over the top) takes the accolade.

Worst Hairdo

Appearance matters almost as much as performance in the modern game. Something of which the follically-challenged Jim Duffy (when he was Manager at Falkirk) was well aware. So, when the goalie, Gordon Marshall, was injured, Jim ran on with the medicine bag, took out some hair gel, smoothed it through the keeper's hair and said, 'You look great. Now, get up and play!'

But the team currently the worst coiffured is Glasgow

Rangers. With Gazza (who is known to fly up his personal crimper from the south before big matches at a cost of £500-odd quid a time – the odd bit is the haircut itself) how could it be otherwise?

However the 1978 World Cup squad took hairstyles to new levels of meaning when practically every single one of them affected a bubble streaked Afro perm. Think of the early Rod Stewart crossed with Jimi Hendrix and you've got it.

Worst Kilt Wearer

Even before he is asked the way to the Italian Centre for Versace and Armani, any footballing incomer worth his transfer fee (and some who are not) gets himself and his knees fitted into a kilt. If his club doesn't do it, then the tabloids will.

Rangers FC naturally had their own tartan created. It is not one usually worn in our wee bit hills and glens. But then we all know on which side in the Bonnie P.C. v. Duke of Cumberland match at Culloden Rangers would have played don't we? Anyway for some reason the colour blue predominates. They made a suit out of this cloth for Gazza. Think of a badly constructed duvet-cover. Better yet, don't think about it at all.

But the least we can expect is that the home-grown stars should know better. Or at least how to wear the kilt properly. Ally McCoist, when he received his OBE from the Queen proved that it ain't necessarily so. Not when the kilt reaches approximately to the ankles. And he is photographed with his wife coyly looking up his kilt . . .

Worst Diet

The modern footballer, who is a machine honed to the peak of perfection (courtesy of worst clichés from the back pages) and trained to a fitness level which would leave a Derby winner standing (same source) would be over a parrot and sick as a moon over the training regimes and diets of old. Walter Arnott, Queen's Park dynamo of the 1880s, liked to have his trainer on hand to run on with a lit fag when the action on the field paled – and a digestive biscuit. Although Derek Ferguson, whose career has had him playing in the Courts as well as for the Clubs, runs him close. He keeps fit for his matches on a steady diet of plain loaves and sausages. With the odd cocktail thrown in.

'Jis' hanging about'

Worst Hobby

It is said that footballers do not have much interest in life away from the pitch and newspapers' back pages. Unless it's blondes and booze. This is of course a slander and a libel.

Derek Smith of Celtic, when asked about his hobbies thought long and deep before replying, 'Jist hinging about.'

But Alex Ferguson, as ever, had the recipe for constructive use of free time when he was manager of Aberdeen. He exhorted his players to, 'Eat your greens and enjoy sex' – presumably not at the same time.

Worst Spectators

Those who live in the immediate area of any major football-ground are inclined to say any spectator is a bad spectator, but since the police got an armlock on the fans, things have been relatively peaceful here. We have been spared much of the crowd troubles of English fans both home and away. It wasn't always so. In 1917, in the match between Kirkintilloch and Baillieston, Baillieston scored and the Kirkintilloch supporters chased them for miles. The SFA declared the game null and void.

Worst Bad Sport

In 1988 Douglas Park, then a Director of Hearts (no relation as far as I know to the Hamilton Accies' ground) took umbrage with the refereeing of Mr David Syme during a tense clash with Rangers. Indeed he became so aerated that after the game he locked Mr Syme into his dressing room and stalked off with the key for a strong tea. It was 20 minutes before Syme was released.

Oddly enough the SFA were not amused and fined Park £1000. He resigned soon after from the Hearts Board.

There was also Cove Ranger's former skipper, Dave Morland. In January 1995 the Highland League Captain was moved to have words with the referee, George Simpson, over remarks made by the whistler on Morland's team's disciplinary record. Soon after he met Mr Simpson in Aberdeen and punched him in the face. He was subsequently charged and fined £200 in August 1995 at the District Court.

That same evening Dave turned out for his new Club, Huntly. The match was refereed by George Simpson.

Worst Booking

When Glasgow referee Mr Talbot and his whistle arrived to do the business in a 1975 match between Goldenhall Boys Club and Glencraig United he took immediate offence to the friendly welcome – most of it in words of four letters – given to him by the latter team. So he booked the lot of them AND their two substitutes before a single ball had been kicked.

Worst Attendance at a Senior Game

Only thirty-two spectators turned up in April 1939 to see the game between East Stirling and Leith. There was no crowd trouble.

Worst Attendance at Any Game

When Larkhall Royal Albert Junior ran on to their pitch for a home match in March 1995, they were watched by a crowd of five. Worse still, only one had actually paid for a ticket, which made the total gate receipts £1.50p.

Worst Mascot

Before the Second World War Toby the sheep was once chosen as the proud mascot and symbol (heaven knows why) of Greenock Wanderers. But he did bring them luck. On Toby's first outing after a bad run for the team, he did his bit and they won. Unfortunately while they were celebrating this achievement in the nearest hostelry, Toby fell into the team bath – and drowned.

Worst Fishing Trip

Tales of Scotland's finer footballers' high drinking and low living are no doubt greatly exaggerated.

Not least by fans who may not be able to stroke a ball into the back of the net with educated feet like their heroes, but who do know how to sink the bevvies straight between their tonsils with the best of them.

But there have been times when our boys' reputations have been well earned. Like the occasion on which Jimmy, a.k.a. 'Jinky', Johnstone went fishing.

It was at Largs in the spring of 1974.

The international team were celebrating a midweek victory over Wales with a wee refreshment. Or twenty.

At 4 a.m. they decided to call it a morning by which time most of the group which included Billy Bremner, Denis Law and David Harvey and Johnstone, were feeling no pain.

As they returned to their hotel Jinky was playing tag amongst the rowing boats and concluded that a sea trip was just the thing.

So off he set, belting out Rod Stewart's 'Sailing'.

Which in the event was just as well because the noise woke the town and alerted two local and sober boatmen to the fact that Scotland's footballing hope and glory was about to get a free transfer into Davy Jones' team in their locker.

When they finally rescued Johnstone they not unnaturally asked him what the hell he was doing. 'I was just going out to fish,' explained Jinky.

However it should also be noted that despite this (and some were to suggest because of it) the whole team went a few days later to an easy victory over England at Hampden in front of an ecstatic crowd of 100,000.

The fans rose to the occasion of course. With a rousing rendition of, 'What shall we do with a Drunken Sailor?'

Worst Punishment

Alex Ferguson, currently with Manchester United, has a reputation as a stern disciplinarian. He is also reputed to have a temper and has been known to throw teacups around the dressing-room at half time if his boys (they are all boys in football) are not coming up to his high standards. Players are not his only target. He was sacked from St Mirren when he swore at a secretary. It is also said that he yanked a telephone out of a wall after some misdemeanour or lack of respect from some reptile of a journalist. But he surpassed himself – and even showed a touch of humour – when his youth team, on footballing safari to Aberdeen, got up to some high jinks in their lodgings. Ferguson first bawled them out and then delivered his punishment – to learn a nursery rhyme and then recite it word perfect to him and the offended landlady next morning. As he said, they acted like children so he treated them like children.

Worst Signing by a Football Club

When Glasgow Celtic secured Mo Johnston, they were ecstatic. Until he dumped them and went to the great enemy Rangers. This was an event which had their fans burning their supporters' scarves in the streets and outside the ground. Mr Johnston kicked, as we say, with the left.

Then there was Tony Cascarino who also signed for Celtic for £1.1 million. Cascarino ('What is the difference between Tony Cascarino and Boris Becker? Boris occasionally hits the net.') was described in one fanzine as the biggest waste of money since Madonna's father bought her a pair of pyjamas.

Worst Nickname

Anything ending with a vowel as in Robbo, Gazza and Tommo, is deeply suspect. It is usually an invention, not of the fans but of football writers who cannot cope with either long words or names. Every club at some time or other has had its Psycho. Just as there's always an Attila in every Rangers team.

Meanwhile, for reasons which have never been fully explained, at least to me – on the grounds of taste I understand – Billy McKinley is known as Badger. But Jigsaw, the name given to poor Stuart Slater, Celtic's £1.5 million signing from West Ham is only too obvious – he falls apart every time he gets into the box.

Worst Autobiography

Footballers, like politicians, always have a book in them. At least the former's are generally shorter and more honest. Well, sometimes. They do not on the whole write them themselves. They are usually, 'as told to . . .' which may explain why they all more or less follow the same formula – fourteen chapters beginning with 'My Roots' and progressing through, 'My Worst Moment', 'My Best Moment' and on to the thrilling finale, 'My Top World Team'. But there can be hazards. As Andy Goram, the Scottish goalie found when he did his bit (as told to Simon Pia) in *Scotland's for Me* which finished with the declaration that 'I have committed myself to Hibs and want to settle down in Edinburgh' . . . within weeks he was with Rangers and committing himself to them and to Glasgow.

Worst Decision by a Football Club

Before David Murray, the tycoon, bought not only Gazza but all of Rangers, he attempted to put his money and expertise into the decidedly less glitzy Ayr United. They refused to take his filthy lucre which tells you all you ever need to know about small-town football directors – and indeed small-town Scotland.

Golf – Our Ither National Game

Golf, although a Dutch import, has been played in Scotland since at least the twelfth century and became such a preoccupation of the masses that it prevented them doing more deadly things like practising their archery.

In March 1457, James the Second was forced to decree that

'The futeball and the golfe be utterly cryed downe and not be used' which order is something that many a sporting widow and widower must most devoutly wish had never been repealed.

We might not have had Nick Faldo either because within 50 years the prohibition was lifted and enthusiastically taken up again not only by ordinary folk but by the whole Scottish Court with the result that when Jamie the Saxt went south to London he took the wretched 'golfe' with him.

But it was not until the 1740s that the first formal rules of the game were devised not, as many believe, by the *Royal and Ancient* at St Andrews but by the *Honourable Company of Edinburgh Golfers* who first played on Leith Links, before moving first to Musselburgh and finally to their terribly grand headquarters at Muirfield – from which the worst blackball ever was delivered. Ludovic Kennedy, whose career as advocate and campaigner for penal reform put him in poor odour with the legal high and mighty (considerable numbers of whom make up a sizeable proportion of the members), was refused membership.

Muirfield's Secretaries' (frequently retired officers and gents of the military) renowned snobbery is only surpassed by their rudeness to those they consider their inferiors – which includes all women and most foreigners, particularly American Golf Champions. Their worst was ex-Navy Captain Paddy Hamner (as in Hitler, as those who had dealings with him used to say) sustained an habitual unpleasantness to the Club's legitimate members (and his employers) which was only surpassed by his robust rudeness to unsuspecting guests, even those who were invited to Muirfield.

There was the occasion on which the BBC top Sports-persons were negotiating with Paddy on the matter of the Open about to be held there. He met them in his room (which smelt of very old dirty dogs, probably because there was always an old, dirty dog *in situ*) wearing an aged army jumper full of holes and darns – dress which would have had anyone else immediately ejected – and ancient flannels. Halfway through the tricky discussion as to where the BBC cameras could or could not go, the Secretary lifted his left buttock and farted loudly, 'Old war wound,' he barked, as the smell wafted towards his appreciative dog if not audience. But then Hamner, a bachelor of long standing was, for many years, thought to be rather fonder of his dogs than of women. So when a member said to another in the bar,

'Have you met Paddy's Sadie yet?'

The other replied,

'No, I didn't know he'd a new dog.'

But Sadie wasn't the usual Labrador, she was the Secretary's new wife.

It was Hamner too who also managed Golf's worst snub. It was delivered to Keith Mackenzie, then Secretary of the Royal and Ancient – and no slouch in the snubbing game himself – when he and other lofty golf wallahs were looking over Muirfield's facilities. Naturally they had their clubs with them. Naturally they expected to play, especially as it was the middle of the week and the course was not exactly packed out. Judges do occasionally have to sit on their Benches. And just as naturally Paddy told them to clear off. They weren't even allowed a putt on the practice green.

Of course the Members really rather approved of this behaviour. What they do to even lesser persons who wear the wrong-coloured shoes, inferior ties and add lemonade to the malt is too awful to contemplate. Except that no such heathen would be allowed within a mashie shot of the establishment.

It was at Muirfield too that two English ladies (they are very occasionally allowed to use the Links, usually either after dark or between 11 a.m. and 11.10 a.m.) were playing a sedate round when a flasher emerged from behind a bush, flashing his best.

'Are you a member?' they enquired sternly, 'Because this is a PRIVATE course, you know.'

St Andrews Golf Club, is, by contrast, the veritable pearl of democracy. Or at least the course is, on which all-comers may play if successful in the daily ballot. Or at least they could. In 1995 this sensible policy was undermined by the decision of the Club to sell time to a large hotel group. About the only thing which can be said in favour of this policy is that it discriminates in the matter of straight cash rather than social class.

The clubhouse is something else again. Don't even try to get in without an invitation. They are, on the whole, fairly polite to well connected Americans, if not yet to women. But then few golf clubs are.

Although less – at least overtly – snobbish on the course if not in the clubhouse, St Andrews has its own worthies and those who fondly believe that life only exists between the first and the eighteenth.

There was the time a holidaymaker parked his car along-side the fairway and departed in search of some bracing Fife air. While he was gone a hit-and-run driver – as in car not club – managed to crash into his vehicle which ended up totally mangled and pushed onto the fairway itself.

It was a new car and the owner was distraught and in tears but golfers saw it rather differently.

As one remarked to another as they passed, 'Some people have no idea. I mean, fancy parking your car like that – right on the fairway.'

Many of Scotland's 35,000 women golfers are only allowed associate membership of their respective clubs. In other words restricted times on the links and no vote – and sometimes no access to certain areas in the clubhouse, their clubhouse. There also remain clubs which do not accept, say, women members, restricted or otherwise at all. In Glasgow, there is *Bearsden* which rigidly adheres to an all-male policy. In Edinburgh, *The Royal Burgess* is equally closed to the monstrous regiment. As their Secretary explains,

'The Society was instituted in 1735 – and our consti-tution states that members shall consist of gentlemen. Back then women didn't play golf.' This is obviously something of which he approves,

'Today we still operate on these foundations.'

Women are infrequently allowed in. Twice a year. Only if accompanied by a member. The Club's trump card is its lack of female lavatories – and as long as the committee makes sure these remain excluded, so will the women.

There is also *Old Ranfurly* club at Bridge of Weir, where it is ruled that the gentler sex may, if accompanied by a male member, enjoy a drink in the bar; as long as they never stray; from a certain small, very small, designated piece of carpet, and not to the room's main area.

Worst Golf Joke about a Woman

Two members were teeing off at Machrahanish, in Argyll, where the links run beside the main road, when a funeral cortège passed. One of the men immediately stopped play-ing, removed his cap and stood with bowed head until hearse and procession passed. His companion was amazed,

'Och Sandy,' he said, 'I've never seen you do that before.'

'Ah well,' replied Sandy, 'I felt I should, it being the wife and all.'

What isn't really a joke however is that the winner of the Scottish Men's Open gets close on £200,000 while the golfer who gets to the top of the leader board at the Scottish WOMEN'S Open wins all of £11,250.

Worst-attended Open

The first Open Championship was held in October 1860. It lasted for a single day, was won by Willie Park and only eight professionals, all Scots, participated.

Worst Open Miss

American Doug Sanders missed a three-footer at the eight-eenth at St Andrews in 1970. If he had holed it he would have won outright, instead he tied with Jack Nicklaus, to whom he lost in the subsequent play-off.

Worst Hole at the Open

It is generally agreed, at least by those who play, that the worst hole is the seventeenth at St Andrews. It has killed more hopes of golfing glory than any other. It is 461 yards of sheer hell, having as hazards railway sheds, an hotel, a road (with cars), a path (plus spectators), a wall (hit by everyone from Tom Watson downwards), a giant score-board and the rough itself – grass in which a herd of elephants could safely hide and graze. There is also the bunker known as the 'Pit of Death' in which the said elephants could be buried and which has claimed many a victim, and the bunker known as the 'Sands of Nakajima' wherein Japan's Tommy Nakajima's hopes of winning the 1984 Open lay buried after taking five shots to get out.

Worst Sweater

Dark glasses are worn on the Scottish links, not to protect players or spectators from the sun, but from the sight of the sweaters which are now as essential to the game as the ball and club. Although it may be a fine expression of nationhood, patriotism – not forgetting, sponsorship – the blue number with the white cross, with which Colin Montgomerie covers his substantial form is not the wisest choice to be recommended for large men with red hair and even redder faces.

However, the worst sweaters might be said to be those produced by Pringle who in 1995 made 200 Scottish workers redundant with minimum notice or payoff and still continued to pay Nick Faldo his annual £2 million – plus free jumpers.

Worst Scowl

Colin Montgomerie suffers from a rare genetic condition which has deprived him of the muscles around the mouth which the rest of mankind uses to smile.

Worst Scandal

The erstwhile Scottish and British Boys' champion, David Robertson, was playing in the Qualifying Competition for the 1985 Open. He was at twenty-eight, top of the Scottish Professionals' order of merit and tipped as the game's next great tartan hope. But, at the fifteenth fairway, on his first round, he was accused by his two partners of incorrectly replacing his ball on the green. His caddy also alleged that he had cleaned his ball and replaced it twelve feet nearer the hole. Although the rules official offered him the chance to replace the ball and suffer a two-stroke penalty, Robertson refused, maintaining his innocence. Something he does to this day. However, the PGA chucked their considerable book at him. He was banned until 2005 and fined £5000.

Although he was reinstated as an amateur in 1991, he remains bitter,

'Look at Tyson, everything is forgiven and forgotten, something which will never happen to me.'

Worst Name

When James Braid won the Open in 1906, he celebrated the occasion by naming his son Muirfield. (It could of course have been worse; he could have been triumphant at Carnoustie. Or Turnberry.)

Worst Golf Course

Golfers tend to think that any course on which they do not break a hundred is the worst. But the nine holes (if they made it eighteen it would probably be necessary to station psychiatric help and the men in white coats at the nineteenth) of Port Moak are not played without a very stout heart indeed. Climbing boots are essential there, as most of the holes seem to be uphill. It is also laid out in such a way that every shot seems to end up behind rather than in front of the player. At Port Moak there are many hazards. But the least expected, which have sent many away gibbering, are the gliders.

Rugby

The 'Futeball' which so irritated James II was nearer rugby than modern football. Although supposedly an English invention of the eponymous Public School, it was certainly played in the Borders much earlier. Indeed so ferocious was the game in the sixteenth century that games between England and Scotland frequently ended with some participants dead and many more injured. The modern game is of course entirely different. Ask Brian Moore.

Worst Scrum

When London Scottish played a local Parisian side on the morning of a French v. Scotland International, they were still suffering from some liquid hospitality but still managed to win every scrum against their opponents – until their loosehead prop was sick over the ball. In the circumstances, the hooker felt this was one ball to sacrifice.

Worst Warm-up

When Gordon Brown played for the British Lions it was the habit of the captain Willie John McBride to give each of his team-mates a friendly punch in the chest as they ran out of the dressing room. Unfortunately McBride hit Brown too hard and winded him so badly that the kick-off had to be delayed for the application of the magic sponge.

Worst Foot in Mouth

In rugby it is possibly more usually fist or even boot rather than foot which goes into the mouth. But Duncan Paterson, the Scottish International Manager, achieved the latter after a hard game against the Japanese at Murrayfield. Commenting on a particularly robust tackle by the Japanese centre on Scott Hastings, Paterson said, 'They certainly don't take any prisoners'.

Worst Sponsorship

The mainstay of many a game is sponsorship, which is assiduously sought by the Scottish Rugby Union. But even the SRU baulked at a deal Irvine RFC had arranged with a local restaurant. Apparently it was felt that, in spite of their generosity, 'The Gulab Tandoori, Irvine' wouldn't sound very Scottish when they read out the scores during Scotsport.

Worst Yachtsman

Sir Thomas Lipton, the Glasgow Millionaire Grocer spent most of his life and much of his fortune in search of the America's Cup. He never won it but was known as the World's Best Loser. Which is probably as good an epitaph as any for this chapter.

And this whole book.

Epilogue

So that's it then.

My choice of the worst tidbits.

But I do not doubt that you, as you read it, thought of many, many more – and indeed much, much worse.

Fortunately it is Canongate's intention to regularly update this collection.

If you would like your opinion, anecdote, gripe or whatever, included then please write to:

Scotland the Worst
Canongate Books Limited
14 High Street
Edinburgh EH1 1TE

All contributions used will be acknowledged.